Zveļaņd изитu

TUFTI
The PRIESTESS

Live stroll through a movie

Saint-Petersburg
Ves Publishing Group
2019

Translation by *Joanna Dobson*

Cover design by *Irina Novikova*

Vadim Zeland

Tufti the Priestess. Live Stroll Through A Movie.
ISBN 978-5-9573-3472-9

Meet the new world sensation. It's Tufti.

Why is it that nothing seems to work out the way you want it to, despite the fact that you act according to your own free will? You might think that the reason why nothing is working out the way you want, is because that's just how life is. But the real reason is because you aren't acting according to your own free will — you are being directed by a script. Another reason things don't work out the way people want them to, is because they don't know how to take the right action to shape events the way they want. Rather than composing the reality of the upcoming film roll, they tend to battle with the reality they face in the current frame. Reality exists only in the here and now, and what is real is real only to the extent that it has taken place in the material world.

You cannot change what has already happened. Yet when you fight with your current reality, that is exactly what you are doing, because everything that surrounds you consists of something that has already happened. If you want to change the script, you have to wake up and come alive inside the movie.

Subject: Esoteric / Esoteric teachings

Contents

INTRODUCTION

Hello, hello, my little freaks!

You don't remember me, but I am Tufti and I've come to you from Time. Time is eternal. From Eternity you can go wherever you like, whenever you like.

Three thousand years ago, I was a priestess of the Temple of Isis. Who I am now, I will divulge some time later. The important thing is that I know who you are. And I'll tell you about that in due course, *for you already know who you are, right?*

You have been brought into the world deprived of a 'Self-instruction manual'. Of course, they taught you to wash your hands, change your nappies... But you don't know any more than that, either about yourself or the world.

For example, you think, you have your own opinion, whereas, in fact, that opinion was implanted in you. You think that you are in control of your actions, whereas, in fact, it is much more important to control your thoughts. Can you? No, you're just little, brainless idiots. It makes me want to slap you.

I know, you're lonely, unhappy, and think nobody loves you. But I love you. And I'll tell you.

I'll tell you how the world works and what is really happening. I'll tell you, why you're here and what to do with your life *because you don't know, what to do with your life, do you?* You see! Get comfortable on your potties and listen.

Let's start with the fact that reality is not quite as you imagine it to be. Reality is multi-layered like an onion. You are familiar with two layers only: the physical reality in which you live, and the dream space that you see when you fall asleep every night.

The dream space is not a figment of your imagination; it is real and takes the form of something like a film archive, in which everything is stored *that ever was, will be or ever could be.*

When you dream, you are watching one of the films from the archive. In this sense, your dream is real and an illusion at the same time. The film you are watching is virtual, while the film roll itself is material.

Reality is *what has never been and never will be*, and only *is here and now*. Reality exists only for a single moment, like a frame on a film roll, which moves from the past into the future.

Your life, or rather your essence — your soul — also moves from one incarnation into another. There was a time when you were all fish, dinosaurs and all kinds of crawling reptiles. Don't kid yourself that you've moved on much since then. There is still a long way to crawl before reaching perfection, such as I, for example.

You don't remember your previous incarnations because every incarnation is a separate life of your soul, a separate dream if you like.

6

The soul is not dependent on the presence of the body. This is just one of the forms in which it can exist. The body is just a kind of bio-suit.

You may ask, what's the point of all these transformations?

Such are the fundamental qualities of reality and life: movement and transformation. A frame moves along a film roll; a caterpillar transforms into a butterfly; the butterfly lays its larvae; the larvae transform into caterpillars, and those, in turn, become butterflies.

At your current stage of evolution, you are caterpillars — small and unpleasant. That's just how you are. I'm going to keep an eye on you.

So, listen. Sleeping and waking life are roughly the same thing. In the early years, you did not distinguish your dreams from reality. You don't remember it now, but back then, you did not think there was a boundary or any difference between this world and that. Then the grown-ups explained to you that the world of dreams is just a product of your imagination, that it isn't real.

In fact, you were fed a false belief. That world is just as real as this. It exists, just in another space. You move from one space to another when you wake up and when you fall asleep. Does that surprise you? Does it scare you?

You got used to the idea, but, still, dreaming and the waking life that follows the dream are like life and death. Life is the dream, death is the waking experience, but not the other way around, you see?

Ok, my dears, let's not run before we can walk; one step at a time. There are three similarities and one difference between dreams and waking. I'll come to the difference a little later. The similarities are these:

First. Both in waking and in dreaming, you are asleep. And because of this, you are helpless in both. This and the other reality exist independently of your will, but I will teach you to wake up, both in dreaming and in waking life.

Second. In both spaces, reality moves like a frame in a film roll. Yet you don't understand that because you only know how to see what is right underfoot. You lost the ability to look ahead when you started to believe what the grown-ups said about dreams not being real.

Third. Here and there, the moving frame can be controlled. The reason you lot don't control the movement is that your attention is stuck in the current frame. You'll find out what this means in a bit, although finding out doesn't necessarily mean understanding it. When you do understand it, however, you will be able to shift reality.

TWO SCREENS

And so, my dears, we have arrived at three premises.

- Both in dreaming and in waking life, you are asleep.
- Dreams and everyday reality are a moving frame.
- The frame's movement can be controlled, but you don't know how to.

You don't control the movement in your silly dreams and your sorry, little life, firstly, because you are asleep, and secondly, because you don't even realise it is possible.

Let's begin with something simple: what is sleep? Remember I said that when you were brought into the world, *you weren't given a Self-instruction manual?* Ok, so you have two screens: an inner and an outer screen. You also have the faculty of attention. This is always directed either towards the inside or the outside — very rarely in-between. So, you are constantly asleep.

When you are lost in thought, your attention is totally immersed in the inner screen. When this is the case, you may not notice what is happening around you and be acting on autopilot. Conversely, when your attention is occupied by something external, you forget yourself and, again, act reflexively.

This is what sleep is, a reflexive state, in which your attention is immersed either in the outer or the inner screen. In this kind of state, you are helpless, unable to control either yourself or what is happening to you.

In this sense, sleeping and dreaming are not the same. *Sleep is an anabiotic state. A dream is something you see, either in the dream space or in the waking space.*

Dreams and everyday reality are essentially the same. Reality is your waking dream. Reality is a dream and a dream is also reality. Why? You will understand very soon.

Now for the instructions: *To wake up in a dream or waking reality, you must pull your attention away from the inner and outer screen and shift it to your awareness centre.*

You are quite capable of doing this. It's easy. Tap your fingers around the area of your nose. Where were you just now? Were you flying in your dreams or were you admiring me wide-eyed, fabulous as I am? What was your attention immersed in, which screen? Where is it now?

Find a midpoint between the two screens. From this point, you will be able to observe your thoughts and what is going on around you. You will be able to see the reality that surrounds you and yourself within this reality. Nothing is stopping you from watching both screens at the same time. *You can do this.*

It's just that nobody has ever told you it was possible, and it has never occurred to you that it might be a good idea. Grown-ups have told you to 'look here,' 'listen to me' and 'do as I tell you'. You were taught to focus your attention on the outer screen.

When something does not work out, you fall into despair and sit alone with your unhappy thoughts about how small, helpless and unfortunate you are. You have chained yourselves to the inner screen as the only available refuge.

Gradually, your attention got used to sticking to one screen or the other without resting in the middle. Eventually, you stopped controlling your attention entirely, so it does not obey you; it floats about of its own accord and you are constantly falling into a non-conscious state.

In this state, you are incapable of taking effective action. You may be deceived, hurt, frightened, robbed, even beaten, and still, you cannot respond adequately. You are constantly struggling with emotional complexes; you depend on external circumstances and chase after good luck.

You know who chases after good luck? Losers. That's what you are — losers — *because the level of your effectiveness in a non-conscious state is no more than 5-10%.*

It's ok, don't cry, my little ones, everything can be put right, and I'll tell you how.

A STROLL THROUGH
A DREAM

In the last lesson, my dear ones, you learned that...

- Sleep is a condition in which your attention is immersed in a screen.
- You can sleep or not sleep in a dream as in waking reality.
- To wake up, you must bring your attention to the awareness centre.

Your awareness centre is an observation point, from which you can see where your attention is directed in any one moment and what it is focusing on. At the same time, you see what you are doing and what is going on around you.

Now, wake up and ask yourself: Where am I? What am I doing? Where is my attention? Right now, you have just woken up and found yourself at the *awareness* point. Here I am, and this is the reality that surrounds me. I am aware. I can see myself and I can see reality.

This is an unfamiliar state for you, my precious ones. You only get occasional glimpses of it. The rest of the time, you are transfixed by either the inner or the outer screen. Now, try and hold the *state of awareness* for at least for an hour and see what happens. You'll find it will be interesting.

It is best to do this in the morning after you have slept well and are feeling bright and happy. It is not worth trying it when you are in a bad mood: it won't work.

So, get into the observation point telling yourself: *I see myself and I see reality.* Set yourself the intention, 'today I am going to stroll through a waking dream'. Then go for a walk, wherever you like, to work or to university, in this *state of clarity*.

For the best effect, go to a place where nobody knows you, on a walk to a shopping centre or an entertainment centre. This will be a free walk through a dream.

When you are immersed in either one of the screens, you are not yourself. You aren't in control either of yourself or the situation. The opposite is true in fact: any situation can turn into a dream and control you.

And what happens when you become self-aware? You free yourself, and from this moment on, your dreaming, whether asleep or in waking, it doesn't matter which, becomes *conscious*. You are in control of yourself, and most importantly, you acquire the capacity to control the situation around you, but more on that later. For now, try just going for a walk and observing what you see.

For example, you turn on your awareness and go into a shop. Say hello, walk about, look around, maybe ask a question and observe the reaction of the shop assistants. Just don't fall asleep. Before you speak, be sure to direct your attention to the centre: *I see myself and I see reality.*

You'll find that people will look at you with a certain curiosity and for some reason be especially responsive and well-disposed towards you, in a way they were not before. What has changed?

Unlike you, the people around you are still asleep. Their attention is occupied, and they are involved in their everyday scenarios, like in a film. Their thoughts are unclear and their actions non-conscious. You could say, they live as if they were characters in a film.

You, unlike the others around you, have woken up in the dream as if you had stepped from the screen down into the cinema hall. At any moment, you can leave, return to the movie, and walk around freely among the other characters, regardless of the narrative.

When you are in this state, you may come across to others as a little otherworldly. They vaguely sense that there is something odd about you, but cannot say what exactly. Don't worry, they're not aware that they are treating you with a certain friendliness and curiosity. And you don't let on that you know something they don't.

Do you know where their friendliness towards you comes from, especially in those who don't know you? To them, you are like a firefly in a land of shadows. When you are in a state of conscious awareness, your energy flows differently. It can't be seen physically, but it can be felt subconsciously.

Just by walking through a waking dream, at the very least you will attract the attention and good-will of those around you. You can make new friends and spend the time in pleasant conversation. But that is just the start. Be smart. Learn to drive reality. If you don't drive yourselves mad first! Hey! Ok, ok, don't worry, my little ones.

FIRST ENTRY
INTO REALITY

Well, my dears, if you have already walked through a waking dream, you should now be clear that the comparison of reality to a motion picture is no simple allegory. You really were there, as a living character, while the other participants continued to move around as if they were sleeping and following some kind of external script.

The comparison may not seem wholly fitting, after all, we all understand that people sleep in bed at night, and during the day operate more or less consciously.

However, you saw for yourself how negligible this proportion of "more or less" is when you noticed your own attention constantly falling into either the internal or the external screen. You undoubtedly saw this and now know how it happens.

From now on, whenever you go for a walk in the dream, you will catch yourself continually falling back into the screen and drifting off to sleep again. Something distracted you, caught

your attention, or you started thinking about something and…
and that's it! You cease to exist as an aware human being; you
can't even call your soul your own.

So who owns it? Who are you taking orders from?

You are being directed by an external script, woven into a
motion picture, in which you are now one of the characters.

I shall gradually explain what all this means, all in good
time. For now, you must be clear about one simple thing. Both
in sleeping and in waking, you are in a film being carried along
in the flow of the script. *You can't call your soul your own be-*
cause your attention is not your own.

The moment you wake up and take control of your attention, the script will lose its hold on you. Of course, you have
to go to work and attend classes as usual and fulfil your day
to day obligations, but not as strictly as when you are directed
by the script.

Unlike the other characters around you who are sleeping,
you see yourself, you see reality and you can *consciously con-*
trol your will, which you haven't been doing before now. This
is your first step into a new level of self-mastery and mastering
of your reality. You have woken up from ordinary sleep many
times, but you have not yet tried reaching a higher level, right?

In an ordinary dream, you are helpless, even if you are aware
that you are dreaming. You are inside a film and completely
gripped by the story because your attention is immersed in the
screen. But unlike the other characters, you are capable of drag-
ging your attention up another level, i.e. waking up in the dream
and even going two levels higher, and waking up in reality.

The characters in a dream can't do this. How are they different to waking people? They have no self-awareness; they have

no sense of personal identity; they have no personal will; they are not free to act as they see fit; they are subject to the script. They have no soul. They are simply templates — mannequins.

When you learn to wake up in the dream, try the following experiment. Ask a dream mannequin this question: "Who are you?" They will try and avoid the question or will tell you what their role in the script is. But they won't say, "I am myself". They don't have their own 'Self'.

In the same way, you could ask the mannequin, "Do you know that I am sleeping now and am seeing you in a dream?" This question will throw them, too, because they have never fallen asleep and never woken up. The dream mannequin lives in a film just like a fictional character, once shot on a film roll.

The only difference is that a normal film is shot by normal people, whereas the film rolls of dreams are stored in the *Eternity archive*. They have always been there and always will be, for as long as *this Universe* exists.

Living people have a soul, will, and self-perception. They can say, "I am myself", although that is all they can say about themselves. Living people are aware of themselves, but their self-awareness, as you have seen for yourself, sleeps, and their will is used rarely, when they need to mobilise themselves to take some kind of action.

And what's more, the will is used only within the context of the current frame, but we'll talk about this a little later. I have already done you a great honour, spending so much time with you, my little fit-for-nothings. Make the most of this moment, admire me, praise me, flatter me — I am Tufti, your High Priestess!

TRACKING YOUR ATTENTION

And so, my dear ones, let's repeat what we've covered so far.

- In your usual state of consciousness, you are characters in a film.
- If your attention is not your own, your soul is not your own.
- You are directed by an external script, which wires you into the film.

I use these terms so that it will be more accessible for you, because in sleeping and waking life, you do pretty much the same thing: you watch the film and take part in it as a character with a set role, without the right to spontaneous behaviour.

If you still doubt that your actions are bound rather than autonomous, look at your attention — where was it just now? To whom did it belong? Not to you, do you see? Then to whom and for what?

18

To the very same script. *You, or rather, your Self is your attention. If you do not control yourself,* the script directs you, whether when you are sleeping, or in waking life; it's the same either way. A dream is the same as reality and reality is the same as a dream. Let's say that life is a *waking dream,* and an ordinary dream is a *sleeping dream.*

A dream can be conscious or non-conscious. In the unconscious dream, you are as stupid and helpless as little bunnies. But take control of your attention, and you come alive in the film, acquiring the ability to act *wilfully, as you see fit.*

You become a responsible, sane character who can freely roam around in the dream. You have already tried it in waking life. With time, you will learn to do the same in your sleep.

However, it is much more important to have this ability in waking life because even though the film of sleep has a real film roll in the Eternity archive, it is still virtual. Life, on the other hand, is real. In life, you either helplessly kick your legs about in someone else's script or you *implement your own.*

The only thing stopping you from doing this is your habit of falling into the inner and outer screen. Your attention won't stay long in the centre of awareness. This is quite normal for you. But what can you do, ugly fit-for-nothings that you are. You need to develop the new habit of *returning your attention to the centre.*

Setting out for a stroll through the dream, *tell yourself that you won't forget that you must wake up.* Literally set yourself this goal, otherwise it will completely slip your mind that you are meant to be focusing on something. If you are lazy and forgetful, you won't learn anything.

Whilst on your walk, you will need to catch yourself as you constantly fall and drift off. Don't worry, don't give up, just bring your attention back, over and over again. Arrange to track your attention with *your attention* itself — that is, yourself.

There is no need to try and hold your attention at the centre all the time without taking a break. The meaning and value of this exercise lie in something else: *your ability to respond to what is happening*. Usually, any event, even the most inconsequential, draws you into the outer film or into your inner concerns. Whatever the situation, it lulls you into sleep.

Now you need to develop the reverse habit — not to fall asleep *but to wake up*. Any event, even the slightest whiff of your environment should put you on your guard. Take it as a signal to awaken. Likewise, any action you take should remind you that you need to check your focus of attention.

You have two triggers for this.

Outer — *as soon as* something happens, you wake up.

And inner — *before* you do something, you wake up.

Examples of external triggers: you met with someone, someone asked you something, something happened close to you, it doesn't matter what, some kind of sound, any kind of movement, anything that previously attracted and engaged you. *As soon as* something happens, focus your attention on it, but don't lose control of your attention — keep it at the centre.

Examples of internal triggers: you're getting ready to go somewhere, to do something, to talk to someone. *Before* you take any action at all, bring your attention to the centre. Specifically before, because afterwards it will be too late; you will simply discover that you fell asleep, then woke up to remember that you were sleeping.

All this can only be learned through frequent repetition like in the martial arts. There is no other way. On the other hand, when you learn to control the focus of your attention, you will be able to control your piffling life. And then, perhaps, your life will stop being so piffling.

For now, I give you a warning. You have woken up in a dream, acquired strength and awareness, while those around you continue to sleep. Do not think this advantage makes you superior. Don't treat others with arrogance or condescension. This prerogative belongs solely to me because I am Tufti, your priestess, and you are my subjects who must listen to me — and admire me unstintingly. Do you? Look at me!

COMPOSING REALITY

So, my dear pretties, you now have a greater understanding and have learned something. See, I praise you too! In our last lesson, we studied how to track attention.

- Set yourself the goal of remembering to track your attention.
- As soon as something happens, you wake up.
- Before doing anything, you wake up again.

If you do this, you will develop the habit of controlling your attention, and eventually, your life. But this does not give you the right to look down on those who are asleep. Observe them quietly without giving away that you know something they don't. *Pretend that you are also asleep.* This goes for all walks, both in waking and in sleeping.

Remember: before entering the dream, you should be well-disposed towards others, otherwise you will be punished. A superior, arrogant, disdainful, insolent, pompous, stuck up, finicky, smart Alec know-all will get a clip round the ear. Not from me but from reality. Don't expect such an honoured privilege from me.

Now listen. At our first meeting I said this phrase: Reality is *what has never been and never will be*, and only *is in the here and now*. Reality exists only for a single moment like a frame on a film roll, which moves from the past into the future. What are we meant to understand by this?

This means that in any moment, only the immediate impression of reality — the illuminated frame — is ever real. Everything else is virtual, the past as well as the future. And it is all stored forever in a film archive, where everything is recorded, *everything that has been, that will be, and ever may be.*

The past and the future are both information. Information is intangible. You can't touch it, but the media that carries the information is material and can be opened. This is how clairvoyants look into the past and tell the future.

The film archive truly exists, although it is intangible, like the ether. Ether substance hangs in the dream space. Both in sleeping and in waking reality, the dream space is whole. In your sleep, what you see is what could be, either past or future. But whether it happened or will happen is not a foregone conclusion as the variants are infinite in number.

What might happen in a dream could also take place in waking reality, and vice versa. In this sense, the dream space is a single film archive. You can watch it and you can exist within it, both in a dream and in waking, but you only actually exist in each frame once. Each subsequent frame is a *new realisation*, an upgrade of everything living and non-living, right down to the level of the atom.

Only the souls of living beings remain unchanged — they are capable of watching the films of dreams and moving along the

23

film roll of reality, together with the frame. So your Self is the same as it was in the past, as when it flew about in your dream when you were asleep, and as it will be in the future.

Our world exists in animate and inanimate form. Life is embedded like inclusions in a material reality. Reality is an inanimate substance. Life is animate and life can influence the course of reality. *Life can compose reality.*

The last point, my little mites, is the most important thing you need to understand. *To compose reality means to choose the film roll and determine the direction in which the frame is moving.* You have this opportunity, but you don't use it, just as you fail to use your capacity for directing the focus of your attention.

You have to compose reality ahead of time, instead of fighting the current circumstances of your life. But what do you do? *You try and change your reality within the current frame.* Do you understand what you are doing?

Again: what is the actuality of life? It is that which has never been and never will be, and is here and now. The actuality of life only exists to the extent that it has already occurred. *You cannot change what has already happened.* But that is what you are trying to do because *everything that surrounds you is that which has already happened.*

The present differs very little from the past. The past is long gone and the present exists only for a brief moment, so you can't change that either. *Whilst you are in the present moment, you are, in effect, continually in the past because your attention is enmeshed in the current frame.* The illusion grabs hold of you and keeps you from entering the future, which is why *the future isn't up to you.*

You might think that you are conscious of what you are doing, that you are taking decisive action, solving problems, and achieving your goals. But all this is happening in the current frame in a non-conscious state, and so, *the script carries you along a film roll that you did not choose*. All you are doing, really, is helplessly twitching your paws.

That's who you are, my sweets, my pumpkins. It's exhausting being with you!

THE INTENTION PLAIT

As always, my precious ones, we will recap what we did last time.

- The actuality of life is that, which has already occurred.
- You cannot change what has already happened. And nonetheless
- You try and change your given reality in the current frame.
- Which is why the future does not depend on you. What do you need to do?
- Setting reality ahead of time, instead of fighting the actuality of your current life.

Much of this will sound quirky to you, as for the first time, you come across a reality that is unfamiliar and strange. It's still all the same — your reality, to which you are accustomed, but somehow different, baffling, right? Listen to what I'm saying, and don't bother me with questions.

Why the film roll archive exists, and who shot the films to capture them for eternity, is not given to snotty pookies like yourselves to understand. Be grateful to the High Creator, that you are allowed to move with the frame for that is quite something. But you are seriously slacking in your development. You're not even using what you already have.

Let me remind you what it means to *move with the frame*. As you know, the past cannot be changed. Forget about the present too. It has already occurred and is of no interest to you. On the other hand, you have the opportunity to *compose the future,* to *choose the film roll*, along which the next frame will move. How?

You have two control functions: attention and intention. We have already dealt with attention. This accounts for your state of awareness. Intention accounts for your actions. In order to undertake something, you must first take into your head the idea of it. When you actually come to execute your conceived idea, your intention is realised through action.

However, all your actions pertain to the current frame and are realised there because your intention is wedged inside it. It is just the same as when your attention gets glued to one of the screens. And just as attention has two screens, there are two intention centres: inner and outer.

The inner centre is responsible for all of your basic functionality and is located in the frontal part of the skull. This is your petty intention. When you concentrate, you wrinkle your forehead. When you intend to do something, you tense your muscles. Your muscles allow you to carry out primitive activities in the current frame.

The outer centre you totally neglect to make use of, even though it accounts for the movement of the future frame. You can determine instantly where the outer centre is located, right now.

Every single one of you has an intention plait. It is an energy plexus, similar to an ordinary plait. You can't see it, but you can feel it like a phantom limb, which used to be there but is not anymore. Rather than hanging straight down, it sticks out at an angle to the spine. It's a really funny kind of plait.

The outer intention centre is at the tip of the plait. It is a spot between the shoulders, only not flat to the spine, but a little away from it. You will find the precise spot intuitively. The exact distance is of no significance. It is enough to focus your attention on it, and you will feel where it is. If you can't feel it yet, read the chapter "Plait With Flow" and then you will get it.

The principle of the outer centre is very simple. You transfer your attention to the end of the plait and imagine the picture of any event you would like to attract into your life. This illuminates the future frame, and what you visualised becomes manifest in physical reality.

You may ask, my sweets, how this is possible. It is very simple, and yet you did not know about the plait or how to use it.

The thing is that you are bogged down in the current slide, big time. You are used to looking at what your eyes can see, but they only see what is right in front of you. And you feel that you can only do something about the things your eyes can see. So where are your eyes focused? In the outer screen.

When something is not going right, you immerse yourself in the inner screen of your thoughts and feelings. And what are all your thoughts and feelings about? Again, about everything you can see and everything that is happening to you. This means that your attention is not your own, and your intention is subordinate to a script that is not your own.

You are capable of coming up with the idea for your own script, it's just that you don't know how to bring it to life. Sometimes you dream of what you would like your future to look like. Yet *the future frame can only be illuminated from the external intention centre*, whereas you are accustomed to using the inner, petty centre. The current slide is your illusion and a trap. That's how it is.

Ok, ok! Don't cry, my sweets, my darlings; don't get your plaits in a twist. I will teach you how to escape the trap, and how to work with the plait. You will learn. Hey! It'll be fun!

HOW TO WORK WITH THE PLAIT

Chop-chop, hurry-hurry, my pitiful ones, a new lesson, but first, a recap so far.

- Intention has two centres: inner and outer.
- The inner centre is located in the forehead, the outer, at the tip of the plait.
- Inner intention accounts for everyday activities in the current frame.
- Outer intention is capable of moving the future slide: composing reality.

You do want to learn to compose reality, don't you? Of course you do, good.

So, let's say, you have a dream. There is a saying in your folklore "it does no harm to dream" which hints that it is also useless to dream. Does this mean, that the silly saying is true and that my snottites have nothing to hope for?

I will explain to you in the next lesson why dreams don't come true. For now, we will move directly to the technique. First do it, then you will understand. That's the best way to learn. Now, listen carefully.

First: wake up and log into the awareness point. As usual, say to yourself: I see myself and I see reality.

Second: activate the plait. Feel it: here it is. As soon as you focus your attention on the plait, it instantly rises up at an angle to your spine and is activated.

Third: without taking your attention away from the plait, imagine a picture of the future. In your thoughts, in words, on the screen, as well as you can, compose your reality.

You may notice that when you activate the plait, your eyes shift into a different gear. Try and feel that: you have raised your plait. Now, what happens to your eyes? They become a little wider as if they are beginning to shine. This is a new, unfamiliar mode of being for you. Previously, you just watched the outer film and surrendered yourself to it. Now, you can turn the film roll independently.

Once again, this is how: you've woken up, focused your attention on the plait, and then, keeping your senses attuned to the plait, you imagine what you desire as if it were depicted on the screen. That is how you illuminate the future frame, and how to make it manifest in physical reality. Later, you'll learn how to do this instantaneously, in a single movement.

The plait works like a film projector. You can turn your little 'I want's and 'if only's on the inner screen as much as you like, but it won't be very effective — practically a misfire. *The projector runs at full capacity in the moment, that your thoughts, words, and images originate from the outer intention centre.* So, if you want to do more than just wallow in your own thoughts, if you want to influence how your reality is shaped, turn on the plait.

It is not essential to keep your attention totally focused on the tip of the plait. It is enough to sense it, like you would a phantom limb. However, you can activate it whenever you wish. The specific sensations are a very personal thing. You don't have to pay attention to the eyes. You can keep them closed, or be completely blind; it doesn't make any difference. What is important is that the thoughts, words and images are in tandem with the plait.

So, my bunnies, my little fish, you're just a step away from becoming Rulers of the Universe. I am filled with such awe, that I don't know whether to swoon or bow in reverence. Go on, surprise me with your abilities! First of all though, you must surprise yourself. And for that, you must acquire the practical skills needed to control the moving frame.

We'll begin with the basics, the fulfilment of immediate desires. Let's say, on the film roll of the day, a certain event is looming, which could have a successful or an unsuccessful outcome for you. To start with, take the simplest thing that will fit into one frame. This could be, for example, making a purchase, finding a parking space, any everyday task at work, university, outside, or at home.

You have the power to insert the frame into a successful film roll. You already know what to do. You wake up, activate the plait, and without losing a sense of the plait, you imagine that what you desire is coming true. Then you can let go of the feeling of the plait and continue to operate as normal. Repeat the act of illuminating the frame a few times over, just to make sure.

You will see for yourself what follows. Keep your diapers dry! Don't wet yourself in the process! You experience very mixed feelings when you understand that something *has taken place that is impossible*. You will find it hard to believe that outer reality surrenders to your will. Usually the opposite happens, and you are subject to external reality.

The statistics for your successful experiments depend — wait for it! — *on your sense of the reality of what is happening*. Your criterion for reality is routine and habit. Anything is real if it has happened several times. Something that has never happened cannot be real, right?

In other words, for you, things are only possible if they fit into the mould of your worldview. If you didn't know that it was possible to ride a bike with two wheels, you wouldn't be riding one. It's exactly the same with the movement of the frame. *You won't be able to control it whilst you believe it to be unrealistic*. So what can you do to make it real? You will find out very soon, my darlings!

THE ILLUSION OF ACTION

Again and again, over and over, my sweeties. Repetition — your pain, my gain! Let's recap what you need to do.

- Wake up, activate the plait, hold the feeling, compose reality.
- Whether it works or not depends on whether you accept or negate what is happening.
- It is only possible if it fits into the mould of your world-view.

You are relatively primitive beings. Nothing can happen to you that does not fit with how you perceive the world and yourself within it. All sorts of incredible things happen in your dreams, but simply because you reduce your standards of critical assessment. In waking, it's the opposite. Everything has to be rigorously reconciled with the mould. So your ability to move the frame depends on whether you can concede the possibility with certainty, or whether you remain in doubt of its viability.

Performing simple 'miracles' will be easy for you. You will be able to create anything that corresponds with your everyday, routine experience. Your experience is what consolidates the mould. More complex movements of the frame require new content to be spliced in. I will repeat the same thing many times, over and over, again and again until you understand. And if you don't understand, I will order you all to chop off your head. I can do without idiots!

Alright, don't cry, my feeble ones, listen on. Once, previously, I said, *the script carries you along a film roll that you did not choose.* Broadly speaking, the film roll is your lifeline, and the script is your fate. You don't choose your fate and not only that, you don't even try and change it, although you could.

You are foolish to console yourselves with the hope that fate, although preordained, is still in your hands. In fact, it's a lot worse than that. You are being led by a harsh script. It only appears to you that you take action as you see fit. It sounds plausible, but it's still an illusion. *Not only what you see, but the things you do can be illusory.* You won't be able to see through this kind of illusion though because you are constantly in it.

Do you remember we talked about the dream mannequins? Mannequins inhabit the pictures of your dreams, like the heroes of a motion picture, once shot onto a roll of film. You watch a dream and the mannequins move. You watch a film and the heroes come to life. As soon as the film or dream is over, all the characters freeze until the next viewing or, otherwise, forever.

Do you think that the characters in a motion picture or a computer game are aware that they are in a film, and that you are watching them? No. Are the dream mannequins aware that you are seeing them in a dream? Again, no. And now I am asking you: *do you know who you are?*

35

You can't ask the characters in the film. You could ask the mannequins, but there is not much point. You are different from the former and the latter in that you can at least dimly grasp the meaning of the question. And also, in that you are able to be self-aware. But *when* are you self-aware? Only in the moment that you ask yourself this question. The rest of the time, where are you? Who are you?

You are the characters in a film roll, in the life that is happening to you. *You don't live your life — your life happens to you.* Neither the dream mannequin, nor the hero of the motion picture are capable of distinguishing the illusion of their actions or, more precisely, *the illusion of action occurring.* So why would you think that you would be capable of doing so?

No, you are, of course, capable, my clever ones, and yet you don't. All the time that you aren't asking yourself the question, *where are you and who are you,* you are just exactly as lacking in rational understanding as the characters of a film or dream. Your attention is constantly immersed in one of the screens, and your intention, in the current frame. So your motives and actions are not in fact yours, do you see?

What happens, literally, is the following. At a certain point in time, you start to want something, and you struggle to do whatever it is. You think that these are your own motives and actions, whereas, in fact, they are spelled out in the script. You might think that you had the idea for something, but in actual fact, this is just the story twist for your role. You are consumed by current reality to such an extent that you stop being aware of what you are doing and fail to see through the illusion.

You have your own mannequins in the films stored in the Eternity archive. When you watch one of these films in a dream, your consciousness finds a mannequin, which comes to life and starts moving. As long as you are having the dream, you are living in the body of a dream mannequin as one of multiple different variants. Take a look in a mirror some time in a dream. You won't recognise yourself.

In the film roll, along which your life is running, it is exactly the same. Your consciousness enters the next version of the dummy, which comes to life and becomes you in the current frame. But here's the question: how are you different to the dream mannequins if in waking life, you live as if you were in a dream?

And generally speaking, what makes you any better than a snail? Repulsive, slimy snails, which respond equally as primitively to all external stimuli. They tuck away their horns and hide in a little house... Your fate is as predetermined as you are predictable.

Even the little that you have learned so far, my dears, is incomprehensible to you because it does not fit the mould of your worldview. And as long as it remains inaccessible to you, you will be free in dreams and bound in your fate. But when, finally, you see the light and ditch the illusion, you will be able to stroll through reality, like a living being inside a film. And you will be able to pick a new reality, like choosing a reel from the archive.

And now an interlude! I am exiting my film and setting off for a book. I'll see you there. Bye for now, snails!*

---

* This phrase sounds in the video.

HOW TO ESCAPE
A TRAP

Pleasure before business, my little buffoons. Who said the opposite? Your pain is my gain, or even my amusement, so!

- There is illusion of image, and there is illusion of action.
- Motion is not what you do but rather, what is happening.
- You are not living your life — life is happening to you.
- You are directed by a strict script, and for this reason —
- You are free to daydream but bound in your choice of fate.

What other insulting things can I say to you? I'll remind you of the main point of the previous lesson. You might think that you are your own master and that you act consciously. In actual fact, you are only aware of yourself in the moment *that you ask yourself this question*. The remainder of the time, your awareness sleeps and surrenders to the outer script.

The ability to show self-awareness for a single moment won't free you from the script. You are characters inside a film and this is simultaneously an illusion and a trap. Regardless of how much you might think of yourself, — *that is where you are*, and the trap has its hold on you.

What is stopping you from escaping? Mainly, three things:

1. Ignorance of the fact that you are a character.
2. A reflexive psyche — "snail horns".
3. The mould, limited by notions of the possible and the impossible.

Look livelier-livelier, happier-happier, amphibians! Everything can be put right. You already have the first thing you need to escape. This is very important, because anyone who is ignorant of the illusion, remains in it forever. Nobody has told you about the illusion of action, and you never had an inkling because such a thing, in your opinion, 'is impossible'.

Now you know. But this is not enough. Let's say you're a snail, and you have learned about the illusion. Would you then stop being a snail? If you cry, "Oh, what a misfortune, I don't want to be a snail!", will anything change?

No. You cannot just come to life in a motion picture and start doing whatever you want without following the script. Here a slightly different approach is needed. There are still two hurdles that must be overcome: habits and views. In actual fact, you don't possess these things, they possess you. But that's ok, we'll drag you out of the coma yet.

You are made snails by the *habit of waiting and hoping for something to happen rather than composing your own reality.* Will it come off or not? Will it work out or not? This is a passive position. From this position, all you are capable of doing is giving reality a prod and pulling back your horns at the slightest little thing.

In order to stop being wet and snotty and become beautiful and happy, you need to shift into active gear. *Not wait and hope, but compose your reality.* Your **mould** is an obstacle, as it tells you that it is impossible to compose your own reality. This is your little house, but I'll drag you out of it, nasty and slippery though you are!

New habits and views are developed just exactly as the old ones took root — through multiple repetitions. Only from now on, instead of staring at reality and following it, you will actively control the movement of the frame. Can you guess which frame?

Not the one in which you find yourself in the present moment but the one that is coming up. As you already know, you can't change the reality of the current frame because it has already come into being. You can only specify the nature of the reality that is yet to come. So your attention should be focused several frames ahead.

Just like when you tracked your attention, now, you will need to *track the forthcoming frame.* For this, there are three triggers:

Expectation — something is going to happen; you are waiting, hoping for something.
Intention — you intend to set off somewhere or do something.
Problem — something happened that needs resolving.

Whenever you expect something, don't wait or hope — compose reality. Whenever you intend to do something, don't rush to get on with it. First, compose reality. Whenever a problem arises, again, don't wait, don't hope, don't fuss; compose your reality.

Frame illumination method.

1. Catch yourself at one of the triggers.
2. Wake up: I can see myself and I can see reality.
3. Activate the plait, hold the feeling, compose reality.

4. Drop the feeling off the plait.
5. If the event is very important to you, repeat the illumination several times.

Try to remember and constantly think about the forthcoming frame. It won't work for you every time. At first, you will keep forgetting. Old habits aren't that easy to unstick. You have to see it out, and replace it with a new one. Don't be lazy, be smart, get on with it or else I'll see you out. You're good for nothing. Nobody loves you except me.

REPROGRAMMING

Don't get all steamed up, don't get steamed up, my dears — mug up! Let's repeat what we've covered so far.

- The snail horns and house keep you trapped in the current frame.
- To free yourself from the trap, you must shift into active gear —
- Don't wait and hope, compose reality. Requirements:
- Constantly practice managing the upcoming frame. Method:
- Expectation, intention, problem — immediate activation and frame illumination.

Compose events in which the outcome is unknown but also compose things that are likely to come true. For example, you are going somewhere and intend to go through a door. You know that this event will happen anyway. Nevertheless, illuminate this frame. Imagine in your thoughts, *in words, and even better, visually,* opening the door and walking through it.

Don't be lazy, don't be lazy! Do you think that you can hide in your house and no one will see you? I'll get you either way. Why do we need endless repetition? In order to rewire the snail mould. You won't believe that reality will succumb to your will until you see it for yourself, moreover, repeatedly.

Controlling frame movement in small-scale events is the most effective training method, as a result of which you will...

– Learn to wake up and control your attention.
– Develop your plait, visualisation skills, and intention.
– Switch into active gear, and eventually acquire the ability to *free yourself from the dominant script and compose your own reality*.

What happens after you activate yourself? You become the only character in your entire environment, who is not subject to the external script. And, failing that, as soon as you lose yourself and become immersed in the motion picture, you instantly identify with it, becoming its integral part, moreover, a dependent, imitative part — a mannequin.

But once again, you drag your attention away from the current frame and illuminate the upcoming frame. In this moment, you come alive in the motion picture and start moving freely, at your own discretion. Now you still occupy the same mannequin but in a totally different capacity. Imagine a mannequin in a shop stepping down from the display window and going about its business. This is roughly what happens to you.

You are still in the motion picture as before, but at the same time, you are *taken out of the sequencing* as if your individual frame could move freely along the film roll. Let's just say, now your 'frame frequency' is different from the frequency of the reality frames, which enables you to *free yourself up from the confines of the dominant script.*

Have you ever seen in a movie or on TV, what a spinning wheel or propeller looks like? It appears to spin instantly or turn

43

in the opposite direction, because the spinning blade frequency and interval are quite different to the frame interval. Similarly, your attention and plait manipulations place you in a different frequency and interval to reality. In this sense, you can move freely about the film.

The yet-to-be-realised future drags you from the sequence of the present when you take hold of that future and try to affect it. The impending reality, though written in the Eternity archive, is always multi-variant and has not been totally defi ned or composed by anyone — *nobody owns it yet.* When someone turns up, who will compose a variant of it, then that future surrenders to their instruction. And if that someone is you, it becomes yours.

Do you want reality to be yours? So, take it, and compose it as you wish. This is a fundamentally new approach to your reactions, behaviour, and existence. The difference is that your attention will no longer get stuck in the current frame but strive ahead instead. Observance is replaced by advance, and passive waiting by agency. You no longer string along with reality as if on a leash, but direct it, driving it forward.

But before your desired reality can become the physical reality of your daily life, you, my head-choppers, must get yourself a *reprogramming.* I can't do this for you. You may not get it perfect, straight away. You will only be able to create what agrees with your everyday, routine experience. Until you finally believe that you are capable of composing reality, it will slip away from you unyielding.

The only way of recasting the mould is the same way it was created in the first place — through daily, mundane practice. *Track the impending frame, track yourself, compose reality.* If you do as I tell you, reality will do as you tell it.

It is best to carry out regular, multiple repetitions until it becomes a habit, otherwise you won't learn anything. And if you don't learn, I will remove your houses and turn you into even more horrible creatures — slugs. I am Tufti, your Owner, and I do with you what I wish.

TRANSFORMATION

Here-here, my wet-eared crook-shanks! That's it, come out of your houses, gather round, and let's recall the previous lesson.

- The method of awakening and illumination detaches you from the script.
- You are mannequins, stepped down from the window going about your business.
- You are still in the film, but at the same time, you have dropped out of the sequence.
- Having detached yourself from the film roll, you can create your own film.
- Controlling the frame movement for simple events is your training and reprogramming.

It is also your *transformation*. You will gradually transform from snails to fireflies. When you illuminate the frame, you radiate an inner light, and the desired events fly to you like moths to a light.

Luminescent creatures, looking forward — that is how the Creator conceived of you. And so you once were before you got stuck in the motion illusion.

Much has been lost, but some things can be restored. Do you want to be a firefly? Then, lively-lively *track the impending frame, track yourself, compose your reality.* Those around you, those who are still snails will extend their horns towards you and move closer out of curiosity.

You won't always make it work at first. You may understand that you are capable of composing reality, but in the depths of your consciousness, you will still have doubts. This means that the reprogramming is not yet complete. This is why training is essential, to shift you into active gear, to get you used to looking ahead rather than down at your feet, and finally — no, not to kill you (though my hands are already itching to) — but to convince you that you really can *compose your own reality* incredibly and breathtakingly.

There is just one little thing. You must try without making an effort, my assiduous ones. Illuminating the frame successfully requires *concentration, not effort.* Can you concentrate for a couple of minutes? Well, just for a minute then? That's all that is required of you. Follow the illumination method in a calm, relaxed manner. You are not permitted to tense up. Not an option!

Why? Because in making an effort, you will trigger your inner intention centre. Whereas reality as we have already learned, is directed from the outer centre.

What do you usually do when you try your upmost? You try and fight the physical reality that is already in place. So, what will you do in relation to the reality that is yet to become manifest? Exactly the same. It's a habit you have. You are all eager to change things to your liking, the way you want them to be.

But you won't succeed in changing anything that is already physically manifest, of for that matter, anything that isn't yet manifest. How can you change a film that has already been shot?

You can only *choose* the future, like a reel of film from an archive. Do you see the difference? Calmly and relaxed.

Note, that if your muscles become tense whilst you are illuminating the frame, this means that your petty intention is activated. You must work solely with the outer centre — the plait. It is not something that you should exert or wield.

The plait is activated easily and effortlessly. Remembering and sensing it, calmly concentrating on it is enough. Next, without losing the sensation of the plait, focus on the frame composition. Visualise the picture you desire with ease, without trying too hard. Your muscles should be relaxed. You don't need them for this; they have nothing to do with it. Quiet concentration on the plait and the frame. That's what we need.

Your task is not to force reality to obey you *but to allow it to come to you of its own accord.* Don't force it. The principle is not to grab hold of reality but to illuminate it with the outer centre — the plait. You are simultaneously the film projector and the viewer. You project the frame from behind and watch the film playing out in front as if neither had anything to do with you.

The outer centre (you must have noticed) is both yours and not yours at the same time. You mustn't put pressure on the plait. Just activate it and then send out a current of thoughts from the plait, not from the front but from behind. Not from the stubborn, stupid, out of habit forehead, but from the plait, you see? *You are simply illuminating the frame; It materialises itself.* That part is nothing to do with you! That's it, that's it!

Why is it so important that it be 'nothing to do with you'? I repeat again and again, my dears: it is so that the outer centre works, not the inner centre. The outer centre involves a completely different instrument. Your outer centre is closer to what is referred to as your higher self. The outer centre is what directs you.

48

The tip of the plait is your hook, by which you can be led like a mannequin. When you have no self-awareness, you are led by the script or by puppeteers, who manipulate your consciousness. As soon as you regain self-awareness, your hook is again at your disposal and you can *propel yourself freely*.

In your usual state of consciousness, you don't propel yourself, just your hands and feet, trying to nudge everything that stands in front of you without taking into account the fact that they have you by the scruff from behind. That is how the motion illusion arises.

And now, you have hold of the hook yourself and begin to move reality without applying any effort, 'as if' you weren't doing anything. What's happening then? The motion illusion is turned inside out. You aren't being moved about, you are moving yourself. You are not doing anything to reality, *reality is doing it of its own accord*. That's how it is, that's how it is, my goody-goodies! The illusion is crumbling!

META-POWER

So how are you, my dears? Are you beginning to shine or do you continue to be wet? Quick, quick, transform!

- You were originally conceived to be luminescent creatures, looking ahead.
- Illuminating the frame successfully requires concentration, not effort.
- If the muscles are strained, the inner intention centre has been triggered.
- Follow the illumination method in a calm, relaxed manner.
- Principle: do not force reality; *allow it* to be.

Allow reality to carry out your assignment. Don't forget, *you are just illuminating the frame; it materialises by itself.* Very little is required of you: compose reality and stand aside, like a third-party observer. Don't interrupt or get in the way!

It is customary for you to think that all you have to do is apply some effort and the future will yield, but this requires a different approach. Physical strength, like willpower, only works within the reality of the current frame. You can fight manifest reality with all your stupid strength as much as you like, but that won't work with forthcoming reality; this requires something else.

You, my little maniacs, must understand, just as I must explain, that there is a flip side to power — *meta-power*. It is, in a sense, the opposite of force, not weakness or apathy, but the power which acts from the other side of reality.

For ease of understanding, take a look in a mirror. From the side where you are standing, everything is material and can be touched. On the other side, in the reflection, everything is intangible but equally as real. If there is an object, then there will be a reflection. Is the object real? Then the reflection must be real too. I am explaining this to you so that you will understand, *that it is not only the things that can be touched that are real.*

The reality mirror is like a normal mirror, only it works the other way around: the image being reflected and the reflection itself change places. You can touch the reflection, but you can't touch the image. The reflection is on the front side facing the mirror glass, and the image is on the other side. The frontal side is physical reality, while the other side is the dream space of the film roll archive.

As you already know, physical reality is like a frame, which moves along a film roll, only the film roll is primary, and the film itself is secondary, and so physical reality is a reflection of the object, located somewhere there, on the other side. And there in the film reel archive there are multiple versions of the future.

Judge for yourself: if the future is located on the other side of the reality mirror, can one somehow influence it with usual force, which only works here, on the front side of the miror?

Not an option! You could bust a gut with effort, but it still wouldn't work. Can you? Yes-yes-yes! You can, you can!

So as not to explode and to have the future you want, you must act from the other side of the mirror in accordance with the reality mirror rules, not the ordinary rules. So, how do you get there, to the other side or the mirror glass?

I have not mentioned it before, but you have in fact been there already. When in the process of waking up, you disengage from the script and practically fall into the world behind the glass. This cannot be seen overtly, and the reason it can't be seen is that the surface of the reality mirror is not a surface or wall as such, so much as an intangible transitional boundary between the object and the reflection.

Everything is the same on both sides, and they look identical, only on one side the image is material and on the other, it is not. On the frontal side of the mirror, there is your material mannequin, and on the other side, a virtual one. When you wake up, your attention passes through the mirror boundary into your virtual mannequin.

It is your attention that moves, not your body, but this is sufficient, because you are your attention. Both bodies — virtual and material, each on either side of the mirror — move in unison. It's a matter of where your attention is focused. If it is focused on the manifest frame, then you are totally engrossed in the script. If it is focused on the other side of the mirror, in the image frame, then you are free *to move*, both yourself and impending reality.

When I say 'to propel yourself' I mean it in the sense that you are self-aware and arbitrarily in control of your own motives and actions. Inside the frame, you move in the usual way, with your hands and feet using physical force. However, you

52

move reality in a completely different way, with *attention, intention, and meta-power*.

You will gradually come to understand what meta-power is when you start to sense it. I would not be able to explain to you what physical force is if you had never tried using it. The same goes for meta-power; you have to feel it and develop it. Your plait is your meta-power tool. The frame illumination method is an exercise for developing meta-power at the same time as being a way of composing the reality you desire.

Next I will describe in more detail the rules and principles of the world beyond the mirror glass. You will suss it all out, eventually fathom it all. For now, don't forget to carry out the method more often.

Do you want to learn to compose your own reality? Perhaps, you don't want to? How could you not want to? What's this, a slave uprising? If that's the case, there will be sacrifices and offerings made, and very happy ones! Look at me! I am Tufti, your priestess. You will tolerate my despotism just as I tolerate the fact that I have to spend my time with snails, frogs, and other amphibians? U-la-la!

IMITATING ACTION

So, my songsters and dancers, let's carry on learning whose tune you are dancing to.

- Not only that which can be touched is real.
- Reality is a reverse mirror: here the reflection, there, the image.
- Physical reality is on the frontal side, whereas the film roll archive is on the reverse side.
- Physical force works in physical reality, meta-power works inside the mirror glass.
- On awakening, attention shifts to its virtual mannequin in the world inside the mirror.

You must be a little confused by the notion of falling into some world beyond the mirror glass without even noticing it? And perhaps not just a little confused but quite a lot. Don't worry, my trembling ones, you actually fall into the mirror world every night when you go asleep.

When you awaken in waking life, when your attention stands at the awareness centre, you, or more specifically, your Self appears in the body of a virtual mannequin, on the other side of reality. In the moment that you become immersed in a dream, the same thing happens. The difference is that in waking, you have the reality on both sides of the mirror, the material and the virtual side. In a dream, reality and the mirror world are not concordant — the material world remains in place, whereas your attention flies far away into other worlds.

Plus the difference is that in a dream you sink ever more deeply into the script, whereas when you awaken in waking life (I see myself and I see reality) you free yourself from it.

Remember we talked about the fact that when you are not self-aware, the script pulls you along by the tip of your plait? So who or what pulls about your physical mannequin on this side when your hook is at your disposal and you are simultaneously in a virtual mannequin in the mirror world?

You pull yourself about. You acquire the ability to move things freely, both yourself and impending reality precisely because you are in the mirror world, beyond the glass, on the same side as the *image*. Only the image can propel the reflection, and not the other way around, you see?

Strictly speaking, the physical mannequin and material reality are not so much a reflection, as a *materialisation* of the image. One way or another, you can manage manifest reality (already occurred) from within the realisation frame, from in front of the mirror. However, the impending reality is still just an image. The image can only be propelled from within the frame of the image — from the other side, where the image is located. This requires shifting into the mirror world.

Now the whole scenario should be clear to you. *Here, in this manifest frame, we have to manage — there, we can direct.*

And now we come right to the notion of meta-power. I feed my hope of even the faintest glimmer of understanding from you, my feeble-minded ones.

OK, OK, don't complain, don't cry, my little whip-smarts. What is the main difference between reality and the mirror world? Here, everything is material, there, it's all virtual. As far as force is concerned, you won't be able to apply it to an immaterial object or space, which is why here, what works is force, and there, what works is meta-power. From this side of the mirror: action, from the other side of the mirror glass: the motion illusion. So, what does this mean?

The whole point of imitation is that you don't have the right to disrupt the established order of things. The order of things is such that you have to *participate in the action and obey the script*. Not a single character is permitted to jump out of the filmstrip or do whatever they please in the film. The script is not the result of any individual's subjective will. It is objective reality, which is something you're stuck with.

Objective reality is such that you are doomed to exist within it, like characters in a filmstrip. You may not agree, you may complain, but there's nothing you can do about it. You may even try to defy it, but nothing will come of it. Whatever is shot on the filmstrip is what will occur. It is impossible to avoid the action, but you can imitate it. You can deceive reality.

Imagine that you have entered the awareness point and found yourself on the other side of the mirror glass. Everything around you looks just the same as it did before. You don't feel as if you are observing events from somewhere beyond the glass. And yet, there you are. But now that you are there, you acquire the ability to compose reality and choose the film roll; not change the one you are in, not refuse to participate in the action but choose a different one, the one you want. Do you understand?

As before, you will still continue to play the role prescribed for you in the script and to perform your daily functions, but, unlike the other characters, whilst you remain in a state of awareness, you will get something more — the ability to replace the current film roll. At the same time, you retain a certain perspective as if none of it were anything to do with you. The order of things has not been disrupted; you are neither spotted nor caught and everything has turned out the way you want.

This is the imitation game. *You wander round a motion-picture like a live character, making yourself out to be inert and you change the reel as you see fit. And nobody suspects anything, neither the script, nor the other characters.*

Besides, you can never avoid the script. It is just that by setting reality you initiate a new one. The new script is not yours either, you are still within its power. But it will lead you to the desired result.

Should you hide from the other characters? However much you may like to stand out, I do not advise that you advertise your abilities. In the Middle Ages, people were burned at the stake for such things, and today, you could get tucked away in a quiet shelter somewhere. You are already a little loopy, so don't be sleepers; don't give your presence away; obey your priestess. I love you so much, I could kill you all!

BEING PRESENT

Hey, hey, and away! Come to me, my cunning imitators and artful pretenders, secret maniacs and hidden super-freaks! Did you enjoy the imitation game? Let's repeat what we've covered so far.

- Physical reality is accessible here, in the materialisation frame.
- Access to the future is open only from the other side, in the image frame.
- You are doomed to exist in reality, like characters in a film roll.
- You cannot circumvent the script, but you can wake up and start another one.
- You change the filmstrip but continue playing a role, whilst hiding your presence.

Presence in a motion picture. What does that mean? Mostly, it refers to the presence of your conscious awareness of being — your Self, your presence as a living, competent and rational individual in an immutable motion picture. Although the film is spinning fast, it is already as predestined, as the behaviour of all its characters is predetermined.

Your presence there highlights you as awakened among the unawakened. You are consciously aware of your individuality and are aware of what is happening. Your behaviour inside the film is also predetermined by the scenario. However, your presence gives you the opportunity to change the film roll and switch from one to another.

To achieve presence, you have to come alive, give yourself a shake and determine your location: the image frame or the materialisation frame. In other words, where is your attention focused: at the central awareness point or on one of the screens. In essence, you are dual beings that can be both on this side of the mirror and the other.

You are present here when you are there. It's a paradox. Failing that, you are absent, that is, you are in an incompetent state of non-awareness and entirely at the mercy of the script.

Remember I said: when you are awakened in waking life, your attention crosses the mirror boundary and ends up in your virtual mannequin. When you fall asleep in bed and see a dream, the same thing happens, only the quality of it is different. In your sleep, you can only propel virtual reality. You can't influence physical reality. It would be more accurate to say that you can, but it is very difficult — not a matter for snails.

In a state of waking presence, you acquire the ability to compose impending reality, which will become physically manifest. (You see, I keep repeating the thought, so that you understand well that you can and should be composing your own reality.) However, there is one thing which you must understand for yourselves. *When you compose reality, you are determining the end goal — the impending frame, not a chain of events.*

Composing reality is about choosing the film roll, not about controlling the script. The script is beyond your power. You are not given to know what exactly the script should look like in order to bring you to your goal. And you don't need to know. You are working as a film projector. *Once the goal frame is illuminated in your projector, the course of events will automatically turn out as they should.*

In choosing the film roll, you set a new script in motion. The script does not belong to you but to the events that have been recorded on it, moreover, without your knowledge. Only the goal frame is yours. The film roll chooses itself in accordance with the specified frame. You don't have to understand exactly how this happens. Illuminate your frame again and again, and you will shift from one roll to another until you eventually arrive at your destination.

In the Eternity archive, film rolls are arranged in parallel. The scripts of the film rolls placed most closely differ only in minor nuances. In composing reality, you gradually shift from one to another. First you appear on a film roll, where the result is close to the set goal but not quite there yet. Then it gets closer and closer.

All this takes place invisibly to the eye and at different realisation speeds, depending on the complexity of the desired goal. Simple goals are reached almost immediately, whereas more challenging ones that require you to 'go far', require time and patience.

Your task is to focus your attention on the impending frame. The script is not a matter for your concern. If you try and set the script or resist it, you will get caught up in its trap. When trying to influence the course of events, you take the reality of the current frame in a death grip, which is pointless. The harder you hold on, the more tightly you will be gripped by the tail, by the plait that is.

Similarly, it is pointless trying to influence other people. Trying to manipulate others is a base, thankless task. It can end up knocking you sideways or even creating the opposite effect to the one you wanted. Characters act according to their own script. Trying to influence them, you fall into a trap again. Don't do it. They will come running to you themselves and do everything that you want them to. More on that later.

I repeat, that you need to influence the end result — the impending frame, not events or other people although you will still try to do so, mainly out of habit. *You always persist in having everything go according to your plan,* but I will win this habit off you as well.

How stuffy and pushy you are! I would gladly dissect you all. I would staple you to watercolour paper like harmful insects, or roll you in a jar with formalin and make an example of you to all other creatures. I advise you to behave decently. Don't forget: I am Tufti, your priestess. Praise me, worship me, do not dare to anger me!

ADVANTAGE

Uh, I am so bored of you! You are so spoiled! So capricious! That's what you are! But just you so much as hint that you've had enough of me! Let's repeat the lesson, now!

- You are dual beings, capable of being on both sides of the mirror.
- You are present here when you are there.
- To be present, you have to shift your attention to the centre.
- In the condition of being present, you are capable of jumping from one film roll to another.
- Composing reality is not about controlling the script but choosing the film roll.
- The desire to influence the script binds you to it.

Once again, let's consolidate what we've covered so far. *You need to influence the final result — the forthcoming frame, not events and people. All you have to do is illuminate the goal frame, and the course of events will unfold as they should.*

The script does not belong to you. It is never yours, even when you think that it is your idea. If you try to change it or oppose it, the script will trap you. The script is like a spider's web. The more you wriggle, the more you become entwined. For the script to let you go, you have to let go of the script.

You can never be entirely free of the script. Remember when we spoke about imitation, I told you that the script is not the result of anyone's subjective will but an objective reality, from which there is no escape. And yet there is no need to escape! The script will work towards your goal if you set one.

When you compose reality, the script rearranges itself to fit your composition, even if you cannot perceive this happening. All you have to do is systematically illuminate the goal frame. But you will persist in having everything run according to your plan, and in this, you hinder the implementation of what you have imagined.

And even when you do not actively compose reality, passively drifting along the current of events, the script isn't out to harm you, because causing harm is energetically costly. The script always takes the path of least resistance, but you resist and so you spoil everything.

You spoil things in as much as you express non-acceptance. In this way unconsciously and without deliberately meaning to, you compose for yourself a worse reality than the existing one, albeit not as effectively as you would with intention and awareness. You condescend to express your dislike every time something contradicts your expectations and plans. That's how you are — irritating and tedious.

So, to avoid distorting reality, instead of turning it into a wonderful world that is pleasant in all respects, you will need to make a habit of one simple principle: find the advantage in everything. Literally, try and take the advantage from any disappointing situation, and generally from any event that causes you the slightest feeling of aversion. Set yourself the goal of reaping the benefit.

Any event or situation in life is made up of the negative and the positive. Reality is dual in nature. Where there is black, there you will find white. Your task, instead of wrestling with it and being single-minded and stroppy, is to set about seeking the advantage in any situation. I won't give examples, just try it and you'll understand instantly, just how brilliantly this approach works.

But in order for it to work, as you must understand already, it is essential that you wake up and shift your attention to the centre. The triggers here are mainly external: someone says something or does something, or something is happening or being done around you — anything that evokes a feeling of non-acceptance, from slight displeasure to rage (interesting, what does a raging snail look like?). The feelings activated include irritation, depression, anxiety, aggression, and fear.

The attention is shifted to the centre in order to disengage from the script on the current film roll and skip to another, alternative one. The fact is that your usual script affects your standard film roll: you give a knee-jerk reaction due to your noxiousness character or your propensity to be negative, or your habit of being defensive, or elevated opinion of yourself, or simply because nothing is going "the way you want it to". As a result, usually, you make life difficult for yourself and others.

On the alternative film roll, in contrast, everything turns out to your advantage because you stopped at the right moment and made that advantage your choice. It is very simple. What you choose is what you get. In order to make the choice, all you have to do is think for a moment and ask yourself, what might be the advantage of this? And from then on, try and follow the script rather than resist it. Literally, take the piece of advice, listen to the opinion, agree, go for something, accept whatever you would previously have rejected or seen as a cause for conflict.

The advantage method is the following:

1. Catch yourself playing out the non-acceptance activator.
2. Wake up: I see myself and I see reality.
3. Ask yourself the question: what advantage might there be in this?
4. If an answer comes to you, accept it and reap the benefit.
5. If nothing comes to you, try and accept the situation for what it is.

The last point might sound questionable to you. After all, not everything in life is acceptable and there is not necessarily an advantage to every situation. Suppose that someone is about to beat you round the head. What are you supposed to do — hold it out for them to take another swipe? Nonetheless, in reality, there is one immutable law. The law has it that if you take seeking advantage as a guiding principle, in life you will encounter fewer and fewer events that are harmful. This includes the kind of events that result in having a blue face and a cold body and lying in the morgue. U-la-la!

ALLOWING

So, my dears, my beauties, in our last lesson we learned that stupid snails always insist on their own script for the development of certain events, and that when something goes awry, they become resentful and even angry, but not in your case, right, my angels?

- The script will let you go when you let go of the script.
- Once a goal has been set, the script will arrange itself so that it is achieved.
- By insisting on your own plan, you get in the way of the design.
- By expressing non-acceptance, you compose a reality that is even worse.
- By choosing to seek advantage, you reap the benefit.

Let's repeat the paradoxical principle — set the goal frame, not the script. It is paradoxical because it does not tally with your accustomed beliefs, that you can and should battle with your current reality, and that composing forthcoming reality is wrong and even impossible. In fact, it's the other way round.

You can't know how the goal will be reached and you don't need to know, particularly in the early stages of things. Because if the probable answers to asking "how?" plunge you into feelings of horror or despair, this will impose a psychological block on your ability to compose your target reality.

You can't know exactly which script will lead to the accomplishment of precisely this goal in the context of your individual life. How could you know when you are a character in a film being led by a script? *Your task is to know the 'result' — what you want to achieve, and use your plait to compose the corresponding picture of reality in thoughts, words, and images. Then the script itself will lead you there and reveal the 'how'.*

You don't even have to be clever. You can continue being dunce snails, so long as you are driven. And, competent, aware snails. Because, once you have set the goal, the script could just shock you. You might think that everything is disastrous. Whereas, in fact, old stuff you no longer need is being cleared out of your reality, so that the free space can be filled with beautiful, new things.

It is quite possible that events in the script will unfold as if 'everything is falling apart at the seams'. And then, awareness will serve you very well so that you can apply the principle of advantage. Acting in accordance with this principle, you not only avoid getting in the way of the script, you move toward the goal more quickly because in the moment of seeking the advantage, you detach yourself from your habitual "harmful" script and jump to an "advantageous" film roll. Even without the plait. If you carry out the advantage method using the plait as well, you will move even better and even faster.

And beyond that, you'll no longer be snails, but fireflies, the living heroes of a motion picture. Tracking advantage is one of the means of awakening. No event should hook you, but it should make you alert, and serve as a call to wake-up. *Your task is to wake up in time, see reality and then compose reality.*

Previously: the moment something is wrong, instantly, "Aaaargh!" You wave your hands about and stamp your feet!

Now: the moment something is wrong, you exclaim (to yourself or aloud, as you like): *"Advantage!"*.

And from now on — *allow* the world to do something nice for you, to help you, to bring you closer to your goal.

This naturally does not mean that you must become the very epitome of Allowing and bend over backwards for all and sundry. Of course, not everything carries an advantage and it isn't always appropriate to allow and agree to certain things. Don't worry, you will be able to make an adequate decision whether to allow something into your life or not because you'll be in a competent state, i.e. I see myself and I see reality.

In your normal state, how do you respond? Either you are up in arms, or you automatically obey. You respond in both cases non-consciously, just following the script. The difference in the advantage method is that you make an informed choice, fully present, and hence, walk into a frozen movie as an animated character, at the same time as feigning lifelessness.

The advantage principle is everything in one vial: tracking, imitation, being present, and composing reality. Performing the method, you track yourself, you track reality and set a course, which the next frame will follow. Seeking the advantage is imitation in its purest form; you are still following the script, but you are doing it intentionally and consciously.

Note that *when you track the advantage, you need to look at reality askance.* Nobody suspects anything, neither the script

68

nor those around you. You, like all dormant beings, diligently play your role and carry out your daily obligations, at the same time observing what is happening out of the corner of your eye. *You are fully present, without giving away your presence.* This is exactly what is needed. And it is very important to remain undetected as if nothing had anything to do with you. Why?

Have you already forgotten why? Honestly! I explained it to you before. I am going to repeat it many times yet though. Behaving as if nothing had anything to do with you is the fundamental principle of 'a live stroll through a movie'. Firstly, you don't give away your *presence*, so that those around you won't treat you with wariness and suspicion. Pretend to be asleep.

Secondly, do not act in the same direct manner as you are used to, that is, grabbing reality by the scruff of the neck, battling with the events and characters of the current frame, and as a result, plunging back into the script, as in a dream. *You are strolling live through a film when your attention is present, and you propel the upcoming frame with your intention and change the film roll.* But what intention is that? The most important thing is that it's outer intention! By looking askance and staying as if nothing had anything to do with you, you activate the outer intention centre.

THE SCRIPT

Hello again, hello again, my fit-for-nothing creatures! You are so good-for-nothing and nasty because you have such a tendency to see more harm than good in life. But everything can be put right. Those who seek the advantage find it and become advantageous themselves.

- It is not your job to set the script and know the answer to "how?".
- Your job is to know what you want to achieve, and to set the result — the goal frame.
- When it feels like 'life is falling apart,' that is the advantage — reality is being cleansed.
- You are walking through a film when your attention is fully present and you are propelling yourself with intention.
- Allowing is the work of external intention when nothing has anything to do with you.
- Wake up, see, compose. As soon as anything goes wrong — "Advantage!"

If you don't wake up in time and seek the advantage, in many cases you will understand what the advantage was in hindsight, but then it will be too late. You will understand when you look back and remember, why and how you pushed against the situation and the opportunity you missed.

Yes-yes-yes, you will keep forgetting and remembering too late, many, many times, until tracking your attention becomes a habit. And why do you constantly forget about your attention? Do you remember?

Here's a riddle for you: what is the easiest and at the same time the most important question that torments snails, even without them realising that it torments them? There's no point in frowning at me, you won't guess.

< *Why aren't things the way I want them to be?* > That is the question! So what is the answer? It is because you are being led by the script, because you are unaware of the fact, because you don't compose reality yourself but simply exist within it, like fish in an aquarium, or more precisely, like snails.

The fact that you are constantly in a vegetative state and only occasionally wake up and realise that you were sleeping, proves that you are being led by the script. Why did you think that you forget about your attention? From absent-mindedness? No, it is because you are being led by the script.

You think that you are acting independently, getting your own way, but that's just an illusion. The illusion of action, if I may remind you, lies in being so caught up in reality that you don't notice the illusion and aren't aware that you are the obedient character of a game.

It is literally like a film. The characters in a film don't fully realise their situation either. I am not referring to the actors but the heroes of the film specifically. The actors may be long dead, but the characters they played come to life every time someone watches the film. Don't you find it strange? Technically speaking, there is nothing strange about it — just scenes from life shot on a roll of film. And yet, it is very strange, isn't it?

You invented films not because you came up with the idea yourselves, but because this aspect of reality already exists. You cannot come up with anything new, that does not already exist in waking reality or that is not yet explicitly manifest. The only reason you have film is that you are living in a motion picture. Film is a model of reality.

Equally as strange is the contradiction whereby you, as characters, unlike the heroes of a motion picture, are endowed with consciousness. It is a paradox — reality's a joke. And still, you have a chance. Although you are fully present and self-aware in the moment that you ask yourself the question, the rest of the time your awareness is sleeping and surrenders to the outer script.

What is also incredible is that you aren't shocked by the idea that you are merely sleeping characters in a script, although you should. The reason it doesn't shock you is that you aren't capable of seeing through the illusion of action. It is very powerful. You simply don't take it seriously when I say, "You are being led by the script." You think it is a joke or some kind of esoteric fantasy. It's true!

And even when you take me at my word, you aren't fully aware of it, just like the characters in a film aren't aware that they are characters in a film. But perhaps, one day, after you have experimented with reality, the moment will come when you will be acutely aware of it. And then you really will be shocked.

But for now... you only vaguely suspect the existence of the script — the phenomenon of fate. Yet fate is just a general direction. You can choose your fate, like a road, but you are twerps that you choose fate in a worsening direction because you see harm rather than advantage in life; and also because you do not really choose; instead you go out of your way to control every-thing, thereby creating even more harm.

The script is much more strict and precise than your percep-tion of fate. It is a program that dictates your behaviour and all your actions on the current film roll. It is not possible to control the script. All you can do is choose a different one by compos-ing a concordant reality.

It is tempting to try and control the script, given your *habit* of doing so and the *illusion* that such a thing is even *possible* for you. When you try to exert direct influence on people and events, you are making a mistake that leads to a whole series of negative actions and adverse effects.

Then the script begins to move in such a way that the clouds on the horizon of your reality can only get heavier. And then you will find yourself like a rat in a maze, looking for a way out, which is gruelling and unproductive.

You must understand that it is not possible to directly influence either the local script or the general course of events. You can only grasp the edge of the canvas of reality and make use of some of its components. Seeking the advantage is one of those components. And if you don't get this, I'll annihilate you all. Dimwits I can do without! I have a button called 'De-lete'; it countermands everything... or erases it, I don't remem-ber which exactly; I should check.

THE CREATOR'S SPARK

Repetition, repetition, my dears, my beauties, repetition is to your advantage! Although it is torment for me... Or not, as I said, repetition is your pain and my gain, my little maniacs.

- You aren't yet seeing or composing reality; you live within it like fish in an aquarium.
- You forget to track your attention because you are being led by the script.
- You were only able to invent cinema because you are already living in a film.
- The cinema is one aspect of reality, literally a model of it.
- The script is the program for your behaviour on this particular film roll.
- You can't control the script; you can only compose the goal frame.

Now, we return once again to that age-old question: why is everything not quite as I want it to be? You already know the answer to this question; it lies in the fact that you don't fully

74

realise the situation you find yourself in. At least, you didn't until now. Is it possible to make things in life the way you would like them to be? The answer is affirmative, the only problem is that you aren't going about it in the right way.

Imagine that you have woken up inside a film. What can you possibly change? The film develops irrespective of your actions. There's no point in trying to influence people and events because everything is predetermined. Yet, this is precisely what you do your best to achieve. The break occurs in the moment that a tiny spark of awareness tells you that nothing is going as you want it to, and yet at that, the spark fades.

By virtue of being incompetent characters on the one hand and having the capacity for self-awareness on the other, you are ruled by the powerful temptation to control the course of events and other people directly, exerting influence upon them and manipulating them within the current frame. You soon realise that this isn't actually impossible and begin to be tormented by the question of "how?". And yet, you can't possibly know 'how' because you "haven't read the script".

So, if the script is a mystery, and you can't control it or the people within in, what can you do exactly?

First: propel the forthcoming frame.
Second: propel yourself.
Third: propel yourself from within.

This is the sum total of the tools at your disposal.

The first one you already know: compose the goal slide. You must be wondering, why I repeat this point so often. It is because you have settled hard into your snail house, your mould, which would make you believe that, 'it is impossible to compose forthcoming reality — you can only battle with the conditions of your current physical reality'. In fact, in life it's the opposite. In composing reality, you install a film roll with a script that works for you, if, of course, you seek advantage from the situations it brings your way, rather than hindering it by always expecting the worst.

We will talk about the third point later; for now, the second: what does it mean to propel yourself? Imagine that you are in a film. The film is already running and you can't change anything about the storyline, but no one is stopping you from changing yourself. Don't listen to those who would try to convince you that you should be yourself and never change. To a certain extent, yes, you can't lose your core identity, your uniqueness, but should you stay a snail? Is that what you want?

You have to change without changing. You will understand soon what I mean by that. Self-improvement does not mean changing your core self. You were originally created by Nature as perfection itself, even taking into account your failings, which all of us have. Where there is no development, there is degradation. It is a natural law. It is important for you to understand that you have to work on yourself, develop your physical and your spiritual qualities unless you wish to turn into shrivelled slugs.

Much depends on self-development. In each of you there is a spark of the Creator, so kindle it. The spark is not of the lord but specifically of the Creator. To lord it over others is another kind of temptation which you must never give in to. Create your reality and yourself perfect. The Supreme Creator does not contradict this rule; he does not rule over you (what would be the point, you wouldn't listen anyway), he creates, and you are capable of doing the same.

How and why we focus on physical self-development, you and I are all well aware. Who needs a shrivelled slug? What can they possibly achieve except frown and complain of their fate?

76

It sounds harsh, but it is the truth and you can't hide from the truth forever in your little snail's house.

In spiritual terms, we must become as fireflies in the realm of shadows. I have already explained to you how: enlighten your attention, that is, track it in time, see yourself and see reality. Even just doing this, you begin to shine. And what if you were to radiate even more brightly? What should you radiate precisely? Do you really need to ask? Well, naturally, with the same things that attract you — *with happiness, love, and rejoicing.*

When you do, snails from all around will crawl towards you, stretching out their snail horns. Even without changing the film roll, people will show interest and favour towards you. The film continues as before, only now, you are a megastar. You barely have to do anything at all; just learn to track your attention and direct it properly. Kindle the Creator's spark within — a most pleasant exercise and worthy goal, is it not?

There are a couple of finer points I will tell you about too.

1. You must 'compose reality' at the same time as doing whatever the script requires of you. First, compose reality; then having jumped to a new film roll, do everything you have to do: go wherever you must, say and do whatever you must. Yes, all this is in the current frame. You didn't think that you could get away with lounging on the sofa indulging in mental imaginings alone, did you?
2. Don't just seek advantage for yourself; allow all other snails to do the same. Advantages for yourself and advantages for others. This should be on the list of principles that make up your personal philosophy. Otherwise, you'll go back to the same senseless rigmarole of trying to control people and events. That's how it is, my angels!

DICTATES OF POWER

Come closer, snails! I have good news for you. Do you know, what the main idea of the script is, once you are beyond 20 years old? It's your personal degradation. Are you pleased? Why not? You have hope; you have me!

- You can't change the current film roll, even once you've woken up.
- When you compose your own reality, you start another film script that works for you.
- If you don't work on self-development, there will be degradation instead.
- You were originally created perfect.
- There is a spark of the Creator in each and every one of you.
- To kindle the Creator's spark within, focus on self-development.

You have a choice: either allow the script to propel you forward or take yourself for yourself, so that you can propel yourself and significantly accelerate the implementation of the design.

Now, rather than getting into explanations of what 'propel yourself' means, I will return again to the question of your obsessive need to control the script. This is a very important issue. It is linked to your paranoia, my little irks. I have to explain constantly, what you mustn't do, and what that which you mustn't do really is. So, stretch out those snail horns and listen carefully.

You constantly want something from people or events, trying to coerce or somehow influence them, so that things turn out your way, at the same time as being tormented by the question of how to make it happen. For example, say you are a guy trying to make an impression of an individual of the opposite sex, so that she'll agree to go on a date with you; you implement what in your opinion is nothing short of the impressive mating dance of a jaybird, but she gives you the hard shoulder nonetheless. Why?

Having the capacity for self-awareness, you ask the question 'how?' and design a whole seduction strategy based on your own perceptions. Yes, in the moment that you ask yourself 'how,' your self-awareness is awakened, but it gets in your way because you're not thinking about the goal but your own silly ideas of how to manifest it. Your imagined script contradicts the real one, but you insist on having your own way and spoil everything as a result.

Unlike you, the jaybird acts without self-awareness instinctively giving itself to the script. The jay has more chances of getting what it wants than you do because it has *only the goal* in mind and none of its own fabrications on the theme of 'how?'. You have never tried behaving that like, right? Well, try it. Just go up to the object of your passion without thinking about it, and say and do, whatever comes into your mind. If you keep *only the goal* in your thoughts, the script will lead you to it.

The only difference between the jay's behaviour and your own should be that you are consciously observing yourself. You need to observe yourself, observe what you are giving your attention to, so that rather than sinking back into constructing your own plan, you *follow* the barely perceptible nudges from the script as if they were *dictates of Power*.

It is complex and simple at the same time — complex because it is unusual and unfamiliar to you to put aside your own motives and surrender to an external Power; it's simple because you can sense these dictates of Power if you *allow* them to lead you, consciously and intentionally.

Now, do you understand what I am talking about? It's still the same thing, *the principles of strolling live through a motion-picture*. The principles are paradoxical because they go against your ideas and habits. In a non-aware state you go against the script, and when you wake up, you are even more impatient to act wilfully.

You have to think and act in the opposite way. Do not resist automatically with knee-jerk reactions; surrender, purpose-fully and consciously. Imagine that you are a mannequin with a wax face, an unseeing gaze and you move as if you were an inanimate, wind-up doll. Then, suddenly, you enter a state of awareness; your eyes light up and ... and that is the only thing that differentiates you.

Of course, you will shine with a special inner light, evoking unconscious warmth from those who are still sleeping. But you shouldn't stand out in any other way; just *follow* the flow of the film roll, like everyone else. Once you have awakened, you continue moving mechanically in the crowd of other mannequins, and doing the same as everyone else, without giving away your presence. Pretend that you are still sleeping and secretly change the film roll.

Do you remember what this is called? It's imitating motion. By consciously allowing the script to lead you, you are in fact *leading yourself*, using the Power and Wisdom of the script. And then everything goes smoothly. By not allowing, you spoil everything. Then for you, "nothing is going as I want it to," partly because you are not allowing it to.

Some may protest: why should I rely on the Power and Wisdom of a script that is leading me, who knows where, and may or may not actually have any true Power or Wisdom. And how do I know it's invested in anything being how I want it to be?

Of course, the script is not invested as such. But there is a sense in which the script will listen to you if you are listening in return. Why it will listen to you and why you should rely on it, we will come to later. For now, let's start by answering a simple question: is it possible to resist the script in principle and is it worth doing so?

For example, let's say the object of your passion has agreed to go on a date with you. What do you usually do when you're preparing for a date? You construct your own plan and expectations. You want events to go according to your plan, and you want the object of your passions to behave in the way you'd like her do.

In reality, everything turns out differently, which evokes your discontent as well as negative reactions and consequences. Think for yourselves; why should events unfold as you imagined them to, and why should people behave as you expect them to? It's not unlike watching a film or television series and expecting the plot to develop in accordance with your own script, and the characters in the film to act according to your expectations. Would that happen? No. Absolutely everything is the same way in the film which you consider to be your life.

81

FOLLOWING

Hey, hey, and away! You have already learned a lot, my dears, but far from enough to walk freely through a motion-picture. We will go over it all again and again!

- The question 'how?' takes you away from your goal and your goal frame composition.
- Wanting 'everything to go my way' spoils everything and takes you away from the goal.
- Resisting the script brings you nothing but trouble.
- If all your thoughts are focused on the goal, the script will lead you to it.
- Do not resist. Observe yourself and follow the flow of the film roll.
- Learn to feel the decrees of Power and to follow the decrees of Power.

If controlling the events and people in the current film roll is impossible, what should you do? Let go of both and allow the film roll to turn just as it is already turning and allow people to live their lives just as they are already living them. Why would you worry about the current film roll if you are free to change it? And when did you decide that you have the right to influence other people? Let them all go, and they will let you go, and what's more, run to you and do what you want them to, but more on that later.

I remind you: *your mind should be focused on the end result, the goal slide, not the course of events or the behaviour (actions) of other people*. You can't resist the script; that's impossible, even when you are being fully present. All the changes that take place in your reality that is in *accordance with your will* are the result of you switching to a different film roll. You can't do anything about the script in the current film roll.

Some may protest that they have woken up and decide to escape the script, consciously and intentionally. Let's say, you decide to do something earth-shattering, for example, to beat someone's horns for no good reason. 'Maybe I'll get the same in return, but still, I have broken from the script whilst being fully present!'

Firstly, you cannot confirm that this — your curve ball — was not in the script. And secondly, so go ahead and make all the curve balls you like. What's the point in that? We're talking about solving your problems and *achieving your most sought-after goals*, and about, why your dreams aren't coming true. Playing curve ball with reality can never lead to anything good. Reality is not to be trifled with; reality must be handled competently. That's what this is all about.

All the rest is trivia, and the same goes for the minor exceptions from the rule, which, undoubtedly, you will come across in the course of your experiments. All these little things are unworthy of your attention. It is better to focus on the main thing that is of fundamental importance. So let's move on to the specifics.

Once you have woken up, the meaning and principle of strolling live through a motion-picture are not to start creating your own tyranny, but to consciously obey. Composing reality and switching the film roll: herein lies your free will. In everything else, the essential thing is *to wake up, observe, and follow.*

Wake up in order to do three things consciously:

1. Reject the script's control.
2. Start to follow the script.
3. Compose your goal frame.

Observe in order to...

1. Track your attention.
2. Track the advantage and benefit from it.
3. Track and illuminate the upcoming slide.

Track in order to make use of the Power and Wisdom of the script. The script is like a river, always moving along the optimal path. Your first task is to show it the destination — the goal. You will not be able to calculate how to achieve the goal. There are too many variants, subtle details, people, circumstances and events involved and all of them are equally unknown to you. The script can solve the task with ease, and so your second task is to follow it.

Following in this case is not quite the same thing as what we were talking about when discussing the principles of Advantage and Allowing. *Following is the ability to sense the decrees of Power and obey them.* However, you don't always have to feel them. Often it is enough to consciously observe the pattern of how events are unfolding, and then to simply accept them, act in accordance with them and show no resistance.

To sense the direction in which the script is pushing you, it is enough to become fully present, to be in a state in which you can see yourself and see reality. If reality does not give you a clear answer, where you should follow, it means, you must listen more carefully to yourself and your feelings. When you are fully present, you will be able to do this very easily. The harder task is to track yourself at the right time so that you wake up.

Here the various triggers that we leveraged in the methods for tracking attention, frame illumination, and advantage will help you. You must use the triggers, *all of them, continually* so that it becomes a habit. That's the only way of learning to wake up at the right time. Unless this becomes a habit, nothing will work. The ability *to wake up at the right time* is the most important thing.

In addition to the above, I give you the control triggers. Your most destructive habit is your desire to control everything: the script, events, and people.

1. I want something from people and events.
2. I want everything to go according to my plan.
3. Something isn't going the way I would like.

It is essential that you replace the habit of controlling with a new habit: *letting go and following*. And now, the ***following method***:

1. Catch the control trigger.
2. Wake up: I see myself and I see reality.
3. Ask yourself, feel, what is the first command saying?
4. If you receive an answer to this question, follow the command.
5. If you don't receive an answer, compose the goal slide and try following again.

OUTER POWER

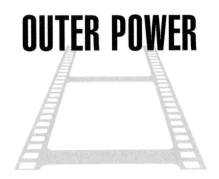

So how are you, my sweet little lambs? Have you understood that a live stroll isn't just a stroll along the lines of "I'll do whatever I want"? On the contrary, on the walk I am humility itself: "I behave quietly, without giving away my presence; I watch and follow". You will also have realised, that in reality, all this is total pretence and imitation. So let's repeat the principles.

- Wake up, observe, follow.
- Compose the goal frame and follow the script.
- Following makes use of the Power and Wisdom of the script.
- Constantly respond to the triggers so that they become a habit.
- Replace the habit of 'controlling' with the habit of letting go and following.
- To follow is to have the ability to feel and heed the decrees of Power.

(Only you mustn't confuse the decrees of Power with the desire to indulge in your own weaknesses and stupid inclinations, my sweetie pies!)

By following the first impulse, the decree, or as it is also referred to, your intuition or presentiment, you are taking the first step. It is a mistake to ignore the decrees. Disobedience is not the same thing as freedom. If you go at odds with the script and make a mistake, it will bring you back into the fold, only this time, in a worse program, on account of your error.

The reason for your disobedience, in this case, is your self-awareness or, more precisely, your self-importance. The reason it causes you harm is that you aren't using it for the purpose it was intended; it leads to inappropriate action as opposed to right action. Your conceit doesn't realise the nature of your situation. I have told you in some detail, that you are in a film, in the position of one of the characters, and I have also explained how you must act in order to free yourself from this position.

In the previous lessons, we have talked about how the script is a program that shapes your behaviour and all your actions on the current film roll. But is that the be-all and end-all of the script? There are in fact two exceptions to this: one constructive, the other destructive. I have already described the destructive exception which is when you fail to heed the script.

The constructive exception lies in the moment that you wake up and consciously compose your own reality. This is the only thing that isn't included in the script. The script doesn't foresee the exception that you are capable of switching the film roll and coming into possession of a different script.

You see how curiously the world is constructed? *The script isn't aware of your ability to change the film roll.* This is a privilege granted to you by the Creator. No-one, not a single living being can do this except you! You are the exception to the general rule. And yet you don't use it!

As I have already explained, the script can even be obedient to you. In what sense? When you compose your own reality, the current script releases you and gives way to another, that of the film roll into which you shift the moment you illuminate the goal frame.

As you know, you have two intention centres: inner and outer. The inner centre is located in the forehead, the outer, at the tip of the plait. Inner intention accounts for your basic performance in the current frame. So far we have only mentioned outer intention in passing when we talked about the principle of 'it having nothing to do with you'.

I'll remind you again: *you are taking a live stroll through a film when you are present with your attention, and propel yourself with your intention.* Propel the frame, but not with your petty intention, propel it with outer intention. The outer intention is referred to as such, because it is not yours; it does not belong to you or take instruction from you. How does it move then and what on earth is it?

You might suppose that the script is the outer intention, but it isn't. There is something else beyond the script. The outer intention is a kind of power, *a driver that powers reality.* Its *active component* turns the film roll in the way it is destined to turn. Who predetermines the storyline and for what purpose — this is a weighty, complex question, and not the one we shall attempt to answer here. It is more important to us to understand what we can do with the phenomenon of 'predetermination'.

You can't influence or directly impact Power, but you can use it indirectly. You have an access point to this power, which is your outer centre — the plait. When you are asleep, Power takes you by the plait and leads you through the script like a puppet. But when you are awake, fully present and take the plait 'into your own hands', meta-power, Power's *reactive component* is activated. This is what enables you to launch a different film roll, one that corresponds to the frame you are composing.

88

We have already looked at the method for working with the plait. But we'll repeat it here once more, just for good measure.

1. Wake up and enter the awareness point (being present).
2. Activate the plait (focus your attention on it, feel it).
3. Without removing your attention from the plait, compose your goal frame.

As soon as you became fully present, your attention came into your possession. As soon as you have activated the plait, the puppet strings also ended up in your hands. Now, without letting go of the strings, direct your attention to the inner screen and draw the picture of your future, compose your goal frame.

Your attention is simultaneously focused on the internal screen and the plait. Attention feels the plait and draws (visually, or/and in words, thoughts) on the screen. It draws not from the inner centre but from the outer centre, which is at the same time both yours and not yours. You are applying not a visible, tangible power, but a virtual, intangible meta-power, which acts somewhere *behind you and beyond you.*

It is nothing to do with you; you aren't doing anything directly; you are simply *facilitating indirectly and observing what is happening. Do not force, allow,* so that it can move of its own accord. Note and remember the feeling that arises *behind you and beyond you.* This is your contact with Power. If you can learn to own this feeling, Power will be with you.

PAPER PERSON

What are we continuing to study? Have you fallen asleep? Do you remember? The live stroll technique. Don't worry, my lambs, it's not that difficult. It just requires practise — regular, systematic practice. If you have not tried it yet, and have only read about it, or listened or stared at me wide-eyed, try it. You'll do it easily.

- The outer, not inner intention propels the frame.
- The outer intention is a kind of Power, a driver of reality.
- Meta-power is the reactive component of Power.
- The plait is your outer centre, your access point to Power.
- Power is used indirectly, like meta-power, through the medium of the plait.
- Meta-power sets in when you activate the plait and compose your reality.

And so, you take a live stroll through a film when you are fully present and move with the power of intention. Failing this you are not fully live, and you aren't walking at all; you're just fulfilling a prescribed role.

How else can I offend you? When your awareness is absent, you are not fully yourself; you aren't there at all. You are just a fictional character, like an illustration in a book. You could cut a figure out of paper and insert it between the pages of a book. That is what you are.

What can a paper person do, to say nothing of a paper snail? Sit like a prisoner in a book, that's all. All that distinguishes you from a purely fictional character, are rare glimmers of self-awareness, when you exclaim: why isn't everything the way I want it to be? That is where the difference ends.

Everything isn't the way you want it to be, because you always act head on, with your petty intention. You want to be loved, respected, helped with something, given something, and so you demand in a childish manner: love me, respect me, help me, give me.

From the outside, this is what the scene looks like: you are standing in front of a mirror, reaching out your hands and shouting "Give it to me!", trying to pull the reflection closer. The reflection responds by doing the same. It does not give, it takes away. In reality, as in the mirror, you always get the reflection of all your mental attitudes and actions. *As the message, so the response, what you put out is what you get back.*

You probably don't remember (for you don't, do you?), but as I have already said, even in a state of distraction and non-awareness, you still compose your own reality to some degree, not as effectively as you do with awareness and intention, with the plait, but you are still composing it nonetheless, particularly when you are wholeheartedly set against something. Reality, as a rule, gives a mirror-like response. *What you give out, is what you get back.*

Reality, however, isn't like a normal mirror, it's a paradoxical mirror. Its paradox lies in the fact that when you look into it, you don't see yourself objectively as you really are. This is because the reflection is the set of physical circumstances that surrounds you — the current frame. Your attention is totally immersed in that reflection. This means, that your Self is literally pasted into the motion-picture like a fictional character or an illustration in a book.

Being a character inside a film, you aren't capable of changing or shifting the reflection in any way. You can't propel yourself ahead either; your 'I' dissolves into the frame and ceases to exist. *You acquire the ability to propel yourself ahead and things outside of yourself when you pull your attention away from the motion-picture,* or away from the mirror, which amounts to the same thing.

Your body remains inside it, in the reflection, but your attention is focused here, outside of the mirror, on the side of the image that is being reflected. And then, you see yourself standing in front of a mirror, and you see reality as a reflection of all your thoughts and actions. Only when you see yourself here, standing facing the mirror you are able to propel yourself forward in such a way that "everything is how I want it to be" in the reflection.

As you probably won't have guessed (for you haven't, have you?) we are talking once again about your *presence.* You are your attention. You are either a living individual and you exist, or you are a paper person and you don't exist. You are only present in the film when your attention is focused on the auditorium, where you can see both yourself and reality. In essence, wherever the screen is, you'll find the mirror too.

The difference between a normal screen or mirror and the reality screen or mirror is that, in reality, the image and its reflection are superimposed. You observe one image around you, not an image separated by a surface into two. But that doesn't change the essence of the thing. Your everyday reality is created by your thoughts and actions. If, when standing in front of the mirror or screen, you propel yourself consciously, then the reflection will look the same. When you do this, you are practically shooting your own film, your own reality.

The first thing you must do in order to shoot your own film, is to *wake up and become fully present.* Imagine that you have come to life inside a film. You aren't watching the film as you usually do; you are living in it. Feel it. Open your eyes and look at everything that surrounds you afresh. Refresh your view. You'll notice that the colours are richer. And now, imagine how you would feel to be not a character in a film but an objective outsider. But you have entered the film as an insider. No-one knows except you. In body, you are inside the film, but in your awareness, you are outside of it. *Feel your individuality, your presence.*

Second. Before you start desiring, expecting, and asking something of other people and reality, you must imagine that you are standing in front of a mirror and asking yourself the question: *what must I do for the reflection to meet me half way?* Obviously, you have to make the first move. Instead of your usual manner of claiming the larger portion of the cake for yourself and harping on "give, give, give...", you wake up and realise that the reality mirror is simply repeating your movements. And if you want to receive something, you must first give something similar. It doesn't actually matter what that is. Simply, replace your 'give me' with the opposite, 'here, take'. Then, as if by magic, in the reflection, you will receive the very thing you wanted. *What you give out is what you get back.*

COMPOSING THE IMAGE

As always, my dears, we dutifully repeat what we've covered so far.

- Reality, like a mirror, reflects all your thoughts and actions.
- Your thoughts and actions are usually: love me, help me, give me.
- In the reflection, you get literally the same thing: give, give, give.
- Acting with petty intent, you do not see yourself objectively.
- To see yourself objectively, become fully present.
- Refresh your view; feel your individuality within the motion-picture.
- Categorically replace all your 'give me's' with 'here, take'.

From what has been said, it follows that all your actions must be squared with the mirror-like quality of reality. Before you demand something from others, make sure you are fully present and ask yourself: *what do I need to do for the reflection to meet me half way?* Obviously, the answer is 'take the first step'. What would the first step be in your case?

Silly snails only consider their actions when they are standing in front of a normal mirror looking at their own reflection. But you, my golden ones, are now so clever, so cunning, that you are sure to understand: *your thoughts and actions should take the mirror into account even if it is one that you cannot see.*

For example, let's say you need love and kindness. Imagine yourself standing in front of a mirror. Move in such a way that you see these things in the reflection. How should you move? Don't seek love, radiate love. Don't look for kindness, radiate charm and be kind.

Try the principle out for yourself. Whom do you find more attractive, the person who loves you, or the person who is needy of your love; the person who gives to you selflessly, or the one who begs you for something; the person who is genuinely interested in you, or the one who seeks your attention?

Use the following table to compose the image you want:

You want:	Compose the image by:	Reflection gives:
Fun time with friends.	Listening carefully.	People socialise with you.
Be interesting.	Showing interest	People are interested in you.
Receive help and support.	Helping others.	People help you.
People understand you.	Trying to understand others.	People understand you.
People are compassionate towards you.	Showing compassion.	People reciprocate
Gaining approval.	Showing approval.	People approve of you.
Gaining respect.	Giving respect.	You are respected.
Receiving gratitude.	Showing gratitude.	You are appreciated.
Being liked by others.	Being kind.	People like you.
Being admired by others.	Showing admiration.	People admire you.
Being loved.	Being loving.	You are loved.

Simply line up all your thoughts and actions with a plus sign beside each one. All your 'give me's' have a minus sign after them and either don't work, or create the opposite effect. Similarly, all your negative thoughts and actions come back to you like a boomerang.

What you don't want:	*Don'ts:*
Encountering aggressive types	*Don't show aggression*
Being criticised	*Don't criticise others*
Feeling judged	*Don't judge others*
Suffering damage	*Don't harm others*
Being afraid	*Don't make threats*
Having an unpleasant personality	*Don't cause trouble*

You don't want a hailstorm of boomerangs to drop on your head from nowhere? So, don't throw them into the mirror! The mirror does not always return everything as an exact copy. The cause-effect relationships of all kinds of misfortune can't always be clearly traced. The only thing that is inevitable, is that the Boomerang will return, sooner or later, in one form or another. Have you hurt someone? Dig yourself out, in all kinds of different ways. Have you done something nice for someone? You will be rewarded.

And now, the specific ***image method***. As soon as you find yourself wanting something from someone, wake up and stand in front of the mirror. What do you need to do for the reflection to meet you half way? *Give to others the very thing that you would like to receive.*

1. Catch yourself thinking: I want other people to give me something.
2. Be fully present: wanting is futile, you have to give.
3. Ask yourself: what can I give that is the same?
4. If you find something similar, give it now and give upfront.
5. If you don't find something similar, then just give anyway.

It is not always possible or appropriate to give to another the very thing you would like to receive, or even something close to it. You can give anything you see that a person needs or that will make them feel good from a compliment to a gift. It is not difficult to work out what a person needs. All it takes is to show genuine interest. From then on, it's easy, just make sure everything has a plus sign beside it.

There is a general principle for image composition: *rather than complaining to the world, love it*. In reality, all you need is love. You know this, it's just that you don't always take these words in the right context. You want people to love you. You think that first people will love you and then you will love the world, but it should be the other way round: you love, you radiate love, without demanding anything in return, and only then does love come to you.

There is a certain type of person, who will willingly use your love without giving anything on their part. Stay away from people like that. You don't need them in your life. Now, come closer, closer, my darlings! I am Tufti, your priestess!

COMMUNICATING WITH THE MIRROR

And so, here we are, my pretties! Now you know how to propel yourself from within, not to wait, request or demand, but to move through life in your own way so that you get what you desire as if you were standing in front of a mirror.

- Your actions must be squared with the mirror-like quality of reality.
- What do you need to do for the reflection to meet you half way?
- Give to others, the very thing you would like to receive.
- All your 'give me's' have a minus sign. These create the opposite — you don't receive.
- Negative thoughts and actions come back to you like a boomerang.
- Line up all your thoughts and actions with a plus sign beside them.

So, what else can you do in the current frame, aside from composing your own forthcoming reality? *Move, and propel*

99

yourself from within. If you focus on self-development, and, on top of that, you know the image composition technique, you will have no equal among snails.

Pitiful efforts to change the current frame, i.e. to directly influence the current course of events will either lead to nothing or have the opposite effect. Trying to influence other people is also pointless. They are characters who are being led by a script, just like you. Judge for yourself: would you really allow yourself to be influenced? There's no persuading you; if you don't want to go in a certain direction, no-one will be able to influence you otherwise. Is that not true, my resolutes?

You can change the course of events in a movie by changing the film roll but never from within the film itself. The only way of influencing people indirectly (we aren't considering methods of compulsion here, obviously), is *to enter into a relationship with them in accordance with the mirror principle.* This is the only way of making people do willingly, the thing that you would like them to do.

Why should people want to do the things or give the things you would like them to? The nature of reality is such that it's not just a film, *it's a mirror as well.* Composing the image has a similar effect to composing reality, only the mechanism in this case is different, more mirror-like. You can't shape the behaviour of others, like you do in reality.

If, when composing the goal frame, you try and forcibly make a certain individual dance to your tune, it probably won't work, or it will produce the opposite effect because you're breaking the rules twofold — you're intruding on someone else's script.

Only your personal reality is yours to play with so you should be the central figure in the goal frame, figured as you imagine yourself to be in your dreams: you are the star on the stage; you are in the director's chair; you are sailing your own yacht... All the other figures in the frame should be in the background, as part of the set design.

Remember this: *you can create your own reality; you can't create other people's reality.* All you can do is have a mirror-like relationship with them. If you want something specific from a certain person, go and see them and communicate with them within the current film, taking account of the fact, that the film is mirror-like in nature.

On no account, for example, should you try and manipulate a certain person into walking down the aisle with you, but you can imagine in your goal frame walking down the aisle with an abstract *(imaginary) individual,* your ideal partner, or living happily in your future home with your future family. Then, your film strip will be replaced by another, in which you meet the person, with whom such a set design can be manifest into physical reality. If you have a specific individual in mind, don't bother working hard to 'shoot a film with her' as it won't work. Go and talk to her, *as if with a mirror, composing your image.*

The most important thing (I'll say it again and again my forgetful ones, over and over!) is to remember *where you are.* You are in a film, surrounded by fictional characters being directed by the script. On the one hand, you can switch the film roll. On the other hand, it has a mirror reality, which is deceptive in the sense that it does not have a visible surface separating the image from the reflection.

You have the opportunity to wake up in the movie, look around, and start strolling live as conscious individuals, influencing reality at your own discretion. If you don't, you will be just the same as all the other characters, my pitiful ones, being directed by the script, acting as if you were in a fog as if you were in a dream, and then you can have very little influence on anything at all.

One more thing you need to know and remember is that unlike the characters in dreams, who are completely subordinate to the script, and unlike animals, which are ruled by instinct and, again, the script, you are endowed with the capacity for self-awareness. It may rarely be awakened, in occasional glimpses only, but you have the capacity nonetheless. And so, you are led not only by an external engine, the script, but also by an internal, driving force.

What force is this exactly? It is very simple. It is the need for a feeling of self-worth and the pursuit of self-realisation. Imagine that you've just been born into the world. What will you do? First and foremost, prove to yourself and everyone else that you're not a waste of space and that you weren't born in vain. This is basically what you have been doing all your life. The form and method this takes are different for everyone, but the root of the behaviour is the same.

From here, there emerges another very effective mirror principle. *If you want to win someone's favour or receive something from them, set yourself the goal of emphasising their importance and help them in the process of their own self-realisation.* Obviously, you will have to forget about your own importance for a while and focus on the importance of others.

It is a paradox, because here, it's all the same mirror. *You benefit when you think about the benefit of others rather than your own benefi t.* If you do not want to make enemies, *be beware of the danger of bruising someone else's feeling of self-worth.*

As I said before, *helping others gain the advantage should be part of your personal life philosophy.* If you do this, you will have no difficulty with your own self-realisation. Moreover, your own realisation will be successful only *when it benefits others.* Conversely, if what you do is of no benefit to others, it won't really help you either.

MANIPULATION

That's how it is my beauties! Once again, it all has very little to do with you! We don't try to influence people and events directly; hands behind your back and move forward from within!

- You can manipulate reality; you can't manipulate people.
- With others, all you can do is to communicate, bearing the mirror principles in mind.
- When you compose your picture of reality, see abstract people and set designs.
- Be very careful of bruising anyone else's feeling of self-worth.
- Strive to emphasise the importance of others and help them achieve self-realisation.
- Your own realisation is only successful if it benefits others.

Don't forget to be present and remember the mirror. Just remember that both the positive and the negative will come back to you like a boomerang. When you are being fully present, to those who are still asleep, you appear as fireflies, all cute and inviting. And if, at the same time, you communicate with them, as if with a mirror, you will be an all-round favourite.

You have already learned many of reality's secrets, but it's too soon for you to switch off yet. There may be other advanced snails, who will try to manipulate your consciousness, especially those who are endowed with power and access to the mass media by the script. Therefore, keep your horns pricked up; do not let yourself be controlled and do not fall asleep.

It is possible to manipulate a character's consciousness from within the current frame. As you are already aware, you are led both by the external script and an inner driving force, although by the latter to a far lesser degree. This driving force mainly determines the direction in which you move, but it is still the script that sets you in motion. However, there are very greedy snails who may try to alter the direction your life course is taking to suit their own interests either because of their intentions or because of their script.

This is manipulation, the attempt to control someone else's path within the film. Manipulation can take the form of deception, creating false values and goals, or playing on the weaknesses and needs of others. Unlike the mirror principles that assist your course rather than disturbing it, manipulators will divert you from your true course and try to use you. Whenever you feel that something is being imposed upon you, ask yourself: *who does this benefit and how*?

Don't get involved in manipulating others; it's a shameful business, not to be indulged in. Manipulating reality, however, is another matter entirely. You could even say that it's legitimate. Reality is constantly fooling you with its illusions. Why shouldn't you settle the score, my secret maniacs and furtive super-freaks? You are sure to enjoy it. Now, let's look at how.

Reality is dual in nature. On the one hand, it is a film, and on the other hand, a three-dimensional mirror. Both are bound to confuse. *The main illusion is that the true nature of reality is hidden.* You can't see the space of a film strip, and the mirror framework itself isn't visible, but if you know this and you remember that reality is dual in nature, then the illusion will lose its power over you.

So, when you stand in front of an ordinary, flat mirror, you observe simultaneously the image (the subject) and its reflection, and so the correlation between the two is obvious. However, the correlation has not always been obvious. You don't remember your facial impressions, as they were when you looked in a mirror for the very first time. But I tell you this: back then, you did not understand anything. To you it was just a fantastic illusion, because you did not understand the principle of how it worked.

The illusion of a normal mirror remains incomprehensible even to this day if you look at a mirror from a different perspective. The illusion of the reality mirror is much more complex still. The space is not split in half, and there is no visible boundary between what is real and what is imaginary.*You are, at the same time, both inside and outside of the mirror.*

The mirror works with a delay factor and it does not provide an identical correlation between image and reflection. None of the messages you put out to the world will work instantly, and cause-and-effect relationships can't always be traced. Imagine what an ingenious illusion this is! The ultimate cunning lies in the fact that reality is pretending *not to be a mirror.*

Still, you can get the better of this illusion. Now you know the principle of how a three-dimensional mirror works, and you know that the subject and the reflection in the mirror are concurrent. So what does that give us? It means that the image you create can become a reflection, and the reflection can flow back into the image. In other words, *you can turn a reflection into an image by pretending you have something you don't, or that you are already the kind of person, you have not yet become.*

105

For example, you want to have your own home. You wander round the shops looking at furniture and items to decorate the interior as if you already had a home. Or you might want to be wealthy — look at expensive things, cars, yachts, spa resorts. Allow wealth into your life. You might want to become a star; behave as if you were already a star; live that life, for now at least in your imagination.

Don't worry if it feels like a game or self-deception. If you are serious in your approach to the game, reality will be forced to take you seriously. It is a mirror after all! Or had you forgotten? Your task is to feel *now how you would feel if you already had what you want, or already were the person you'd like to be.* You have to fake it and live out the game. It's make-believe, but it is not a joke. It's no joke, you see?

So what happens next?

Gradually, *the picture of reality will attune itself to your make-believe.* Reality loves to create illusions, but can't stand being fed them. It will find a way of turning the illusion you have created into reality.

COMPOSING
THE REFLECTION

So, my conniving hypocrites and conspiring pretenders, you understand that strolling live through a motion picture is not just a matter of make-believe, it is also a masquerade?

- Manipulating a person's consciousness is paramount to controlling their course in life.
- Ask yourself: whom does this benefit and how?
- The nature of reality is two-fold and furtive: it is a movie and a three-dimensional mirror.
- In reality, you are simultaneously inside and outside the mirror.
- Feel it and fake it as if you already had what you desire.
- Reality will gradually bring itself into alignment with your make-believe.

Yes, it's playing a game with reality, but the game is real and quite serious. And yes, it's a masquerade. Reality has many different faces and you too have your own masks for reality: imi-

107

tation and being present, allowing and tracking, observing and composing, the subject's image and its reflection. All this is on the one hand make-believe, and on the other hand, very real.

Now we'll discuss in more detail the meaning of what we talked about in our previous lesson: *you can turn a reflection into an image (the subject), by pretending that you have something you don't yet have or that you are someone, who you have not yet become.*

This means that you are capable of generating an image, as well as a reflection. In the first case, the image appears as a reflection, whereas in the second, the opposite is true, the reflection appears as the image.

Why does one appear as the other and why is this process two-way? It is because in the mirror, the image and its reflection are concurrent. The image in the context of your ability to shape reality, is your thoughts and actions. The reflection is also you and your entire environment, i.e. your physical reality.

First (direct) process: what you put out is what you get back; what you give is what you receive; and who you really are is what you have.

Second (opposite) process: as the game, so the reality; what you imitate is what you get; who you pretend to be is who you will become.

Directly: the image appears as the reflection. Composing the image is your way of putting a message out to reality. What you put out is what you have.

Reversed: the reflection appears as the image. Make-believe and imitation is your way of composing the reflection. Who you have pretended to be, is in reality, the person you have become.

All these exercises with the mirror are what is being referred to when we say, 'moving from within'.

What is the difference between shaping an image or a reflection and shaping reality? When you compose an image or a reflection, you are working with the mirror. When you shape reality, you illuminate the upcoming frame. In each case, you are using a different aspect of the nature of reality. In the first-case — the mirror, in the second — the film. The technique is different in each case, but the result is the same — what you desire becomes manifested in physical reality.

You may question whether faking it is really enough to somehow miraculously turn something into reality. Don't worry, my timid little ones, reality is quite pliable. It will find its ways and hows, for this is a film in many variations, and the illusory mirror, is also an illusion, which can be shaped and controlled; all you have to do is remember, and use the right approach.

The first essential condition: it's a very serious game. When a good actor plays a role, they become transformed into their character; they literally live it, because playing a role is a serious game. Your task is to perform the reverse path. From the character that you currently are, which you aren't satisfied with, you should become the actor, playing the role of an imaginary character. You must live your role to such a degree, that you genuinely are transformed into that being. This is the reverse process, in which the reflection is transformed into the image of the subject.

The second essential condition: the game needs to be consistent. The mirror of reality does not respond instantly. It has a time delay factor, so in order to create change, you have to act purposefully, methodically and regularly. Once you have begun playing with reality, you must be patient. At first you have to act blindly, without relying on instant results. Results will most assuredly appear, but only if reality, observing your game, is the first to lose patience.

Composing a reflection means creating your own illusion for reality. If there is something you want, pretend that you already have it. If there is someone you want to become, behave as if you already were that person. Be in the role, take it seriously and live it *like a professional actor.* Live it in your thoughts, in virtual space, and where possible, in your actions, in reality, until you totally believe in the illusion you have created. As soon as you believe it, reality will believe it too. Then a miracle will happen.

And now **the reflection method**, again and again, over and over, my boring ones!

1. Catch yourself thinking: I want something or I want to be a certain type of person.
2. Become fully present: wanting is futile, you have to start composing.
3. Fake it and behave as if you had already achieved what you desire.

It doesn't matter how exactly you fake it, that's for you to decide. But be inventive! That's something you don't need my advice on. The more creative you are, the more effective you will be.

The technique of image composition is mostly used in relation to people; the technique of composing the reflection, mostly in relation to reality. It is better not to pretend with other people but to be sincere and to be yourself. But you can pretend as much as you like in front of the reality mirror, within limits of course *and, without losing a sense of reality.*

Remember that playing with the mirror and the upcoming frame alone is not enough. You also need **do everything** that is required of you to realise the goal in the current frame, that is, to take concrete action, and not just lie around on the sofa dreaming.

FATAL DILEMMA

In the last lesson, I, divine and wonderful as I am, told you, insignificant and hateful as you are, that reality itself is an illusion. That does not mean that it is fake. To itself, reality is real. It is only to you that reality is illusory and uncontrollable, because you aren't aware of the properties of reality or how to use them.

It is like not knowing that you can ride a horse. If you don't ride the horse, it will gallop away with you, and won't be yours to control. Reality isn't yours to control either; it has nothing to do with you. But if you are aware of its properties and use them, the illusion will become subject to your will; it will be yours.

- The image is the subject of your thoughts and actions; this is always primary.
- The reflection is you, your environment, your physical life.
- The image is the message you send out: what you give out is what you get back.

- Make-believe and imitation is your way of composing the reflection.
- What you imitate is what you get; who you pretend to be is who you will become.
- Prerequisites: it's a game, but a systematic game taken with absolute seriousness.
- The image and the reflection become each other.

They flow into each other in the sense that the image of your thoughts and actions has an effect on your entire life, and life, in turn, affects your behaviour and thinking. If you let this process take its own course, you and your life will gradually deteriorate, as is usually the case. This is because when you observe such a life, your thoughts become more dismal; and the more dismal your thoughts, the worse life becomes, and so on, via the feedback loop.

This is the fatal dilemma: do you want to be happy and beautiful or do you want to be devoured by a hippo? If you don't want the hippo, then, quick, quick, stop suffering, stop suffering, and get composing, — get composing!

You can compose an image, a reflection and reality separately, depending on the circumstances, or you can integrate these techniques. For example, to achieve a certain goal, you can systematically compose the goal frame, at the same time pretending that you have already achieved your goal; and at the same time, making sure that all your thoughts and actions are marked with a plus sign beside them.

The knack of using all the techniques together will come with practise. To build up experience, you should regularly and repeatedly practice strolling live through a film. You should constantly track yourself, wake up and carry out the method.

You may wonder whether so many different methods are really necessary. They are and the reason for this is that the methods help you develop new habits. Because you are ruled by your habits, without them, you are not capable of controlling yourself, or, consequently, reality. You live according to the habits you have developed. So you have to create the kind of habits that will work for you.

You cannot stay being fully present all the time. You do everything by habits when you are in a non-conscious state. This means that if you are not sufficiently present and self-aware, you need to be able to carry out the right actions automatically. And for this to happen, at the very least, you must...

replace the habit of wanting with the habit of giving.
replace the habit of rejecting with the habit of accepting.
replace the habit of dropping off with the habit of waking up.

These methods release you from the script, animate you in the movie, and at the same time, make beneficial practices second nature. The proverb affirms: "better good habits than good manners". The most beneficial habit is this: *don't want things of reality; visualise and compose reality*. This is the main thing, and it has equally important derivatives:

Don't be afraid, compose instead.
Don't wait, compose instead.
Don't hope, compose instead.
Don't lament, compose instead.

As soon as you catch yourself waiting for something, hoping for something, being anxious or burdened by something, wake up and be aware: you are being led by the external script, not your own script and that is what is really burdening you. You feel subconsciously that you are not free, that you are dependent on reality, that you are limited by circumstances like a character is limited by a plot. You may sense it, but you cannot do anything about it. Because you are not fully aware you can do nothing except wait and hope.

Now that you know that you can release yourself from the script and jump to another film roll, the habit of waiting and hoping makes no sense at all. Instead, you should wake up and compose a picture of the reality you want. In the same way, it is futile to waste time lamenting your sorry lot. You have to wake up and derive benefit from the situation. Divination is also futile. You have to wake up and follow the dictates of Power. For every situation, there is a corresponding trigger and method that can be applied.

You have to get to the point where you truly know that holding out for something to happen or not happen, to work out or not to work out, is foolish and pointless. It is within the power of your will to compose an image, a reflection, or reality, or all of these things at the same time. Compose whatever it is that you want. Do it yourself, do it! Compose, and compose some more! And don't forget to admire me! You are my favourites, captivating and entrancing, and I am your Tufti, magnificent and stunning!

YOU ARE AMAZING

In one of our previous lessons, I stood here, magnificent and resplendent as I am, before you lot, useless and unattractive as you are, and uttered the brilliant phrase that reality pretends not to be a mirror. Similarly, reality pretends not to be a motion picture. This comes easily to reality.

Try telling your neighbours, sleeping snails, that their life is a film. Or in a dream, some time, try telling the dream mannequins that you are sleeping and that you are seeing them in a dream. Neither the former nor the latter will understand or believe you. There is no point in trying to persuade them. Convince yourself properly first! You need reprogramming!

- You sense, that you are being led by an external script, — this is what burdens you.
- The different types of composition can be applied individually or together.
- Strolling live has to be practiced constantly and consistently.
- The methods instil new habits that work for you.
- Holding out for something that may or may not happen, is foolish and futile.

- Don't want, wait or hope; compose your own reality instead.

Last time we racked our brains over a highly complex dilemma. Which is better: to live with misfortune or to happily be eaten alive? No, that wasn't it. Which is better: a charming hippopotamus or a despotic priestess? No, that wasn't it. A hippo, studious and gentle, or a maleficent and all ways round malevolent Priestess? But you know me, I am not really evil; I am super kind, I could eat you all up myself. I am merciful and good!

It is your lot that are miserable and unfortunate. And why? Because it isn't your movie that is playing in your life. It's not just me that doesn't like you; you don't like yourselves and that's another reason for your ills.

Why isn't your movie playing in your life? Because you don't understand that life is a film in the first place. You might know this in principle, but you are not fully aware of it. So, I remind you again and again of where you are, my tiresome little ones, until you really get it.

In normal life, you are used to watching a film on a screen. Now, imagine that you are inside the movie. Feel it. Here you are at the mercy of the script, but you have a degree of freedom, nonetheless. *When you are being fully present, you are capable of carrying out actions that are not foreseen by the current script.* You receive a degree of freedom in the moment you wake up. In this moment, you are capable of giving yourself a shakeup and setting up a different film roll. Later, you'll be back in the hands of the script again, but, if the moment is not lost, your film will start playing in the meantime.

The reason you don't you like yourself is that all the screens and printed covers illustrate the ideals of beauty, success, and happiness. And you, my faithful ones, are taken in by these illusions, obediently trying to become something else that isn't really you, every time finding that you don't fit the norm. In actual fact, beauty, success, and happiness can never be standardised; they are things with a very individual cut. Still, you prefer to believe in the illusion and try to keep up with it.

Have you ever wondered why it is so difficult for you to remake or improve yourself? Have you ever asked yourself why, on so many occasions, you've planned to turn over a new leaf on Monday and never actually managed it? It is because you are lazy? No. It's because you are being led by a script. *Why should the script change, simply because you have decided to turn over a new leaf?* Your desires are your course, but that course is not written into the script and so has no effect on it whatsoever.

Have you ever wondered why, when you leave the cinema all inspired, you think: I can do that too! You think, I will become like him or like her! Sometimes you even try to emulate them, but you don't become like them in the end. The reason for this is that although you wanted to be like that person, you didn't know about the emulation technique, which we have called *imitation, and that the technique does actually work,* at least it works when it is carried out correctly.

First of all, you have to totally believe that imitation is possible in principle. *It is possible to compose not only reality but yourself, your own new mannequin. And at the same time, the mannequin will change. By shifting the film roll and the reflection in turn, you will change and become the way you dreamed of seeing yourself.*

Do you find this hard to believe, my wary ones? This is because you have already tried something similar and it didn't work; you have always tried and failed because you were working in passive mode. In your dreams, you draw yourself in rays of glory, but this is ineffective, as you now know; you have to use the plait. You tried emulating your idols, but you weren't serious about your approach because you thought you could compose the reflection directly. You were not consistent because when you did not see instant results, you decided to give up.

It is totally realistic to improve and remake yourself, only, in order to do so, you must listen to your priestess! When you propel yourself from within, you can be amazing. Moving from within, you can become great. And when you move in this way simultaneously moving your own film, you can transform your entire life turn into splendour. Um...I envy you! And why am I telling you all this?

And now, *the integrated propelling — strolling method*

1. Compose a new reality and yourself within it.
2. Pretend that you already live in this reality and have already embodied that new self.
3. And, of course, act, create, fan the Creator's Spark within.

This is what we talked about earlier; it is what you are capable of doing inside the film: propel the forthcoming frame, propel yourself, propel yourself from within. Take it all seriously, practice consistently and for a relatively long period of time — always. Then, from film roll to film roll, from reflection to reflection, your mannequin and your life will begin to change. You will see change; of that there is no doubt.

118

YOU
ARE PERFECT

I hope you have understood at least some of this, my dear snails. If you are unhappy and unfortunate, if nobody likes you and nobody needs you, if your situation is desperate and you can see no way out, know, that there is a way out.

Don't be envious of what you see in others; and don't be discouraged by what you see in yourself; be like fireflies and propel yourself from within. Don't look at your reality as something that is beyond your control; instead, compose a new one. Shift your forthcoming reality by using the plait, and shift your current reality by propelling yourself forward using the image you visualise, and the reflection technique.

- You don't like yourselves, because you compare yourself to other people's "norms".
- Beauty, success, and happiness are unique to every individual.
- It's hard for you to remake yourself, because you are being led by the script.

119

- Your desires are not written into the script and have no effect upon it.
- By composing your own reflection, you can change yourself, your mannequin.
- Propel and stroll: an integrated technique taken seriously, consistently for always.

In the last lesson, we looked at the following idea: not only can you compose your own reality, you can compose yourself as well, your new mannequin. If you weren't asleep, you would see that this is possible. So, what do I mean by this?

Let me remind you. You have your own mannequins in the films rolls, which are stored in the Eternity archive. When you see one of these film rolls in a dream, your consciousness finds your corresponding mannequin, and then it comes to life and starts to move. For as long as you dream this dream, you occupy the body of the dream mannequin, as one *of your many potential variants*.

The same thing happens in physical reality — in the film rolls, according to which your everyday life is moving. On each new film roll, your consciousness enters the next version of the mannequin, which then comes to life and becomes you in the current frame.

Do you remember I once said that if you look in a mirror whilst you are dreaming, you might not recognise yourself? You do not just have one mannequin that is characteristic of your being, but a whole bunch of them i.e. one particular or very specific mannequin for each film roll. In all the films stored nearby, you are pretty much the same, and are recognisable as you. In films that are stored far away from the current film roll, you are completely different.

It's not about the fact that once you were young, and then you aged, or once you were slim, and then you put on weight.

The mannequin can change right now in a very short period of time. You are capable of changing very quickly, to the point of spectacularly changing your outer appearance. You can also change qualities and skills such as self-confidence, charm, ability to communicate, courage, intelligence, and professionalism.

But before I explain how to do this, I want to explain something. Changing yourself doesn't mean judging and rejecting yourself or chucking out the old you. We are talking about self-development, especially if you are one of those rare exceptions who like themselves just the way they are and doesn't particularly feel the need to change. Even if that is the case, you have to keep developing, otherwise you'll go down the slippery slope of deterioration.

You have to change yourself, without changing your core identity, your principles, beliefs, and philosophy of life. Making yourself a better person doesn't mean compromising your identity. You can work on self-development at the same time as retaining your true self. It's not so much a matter of remaking yourself, as kindling the Creator's Spark. Don't force yourself to conform to the norms of others; create your own 'norms', so that other snails look to you with envy. You can create your own norms if you accept your own uniqueness. *Uniqueness may be all you have, but* **it is more than enough**.

Uniqueness is perfect unto itself because there is nothing of its kind anywhere else. How can something which cannot be found anywhere else or in anyone else not be very valuable? It is an advantage, which you can either use or chuck to the back of a dusty, old cupboard. It is all a matter of choice.

However, it is not easy to accept that you are unique, self-sufficient and perfect, just as you are, just as becoming aware that you are inside a motion picture is not easy. You will notice that when there is something about yourself that you categorically dislike, it is almost impossible to convince you that this very thing could become to your advantage.

For example, from the point of view of accepted norms, something in your appearance, your personality or manner might be considered a shortcoming. But all shortcomings have one paradoxical aspect. If you accept a shortcoming, it becomes a valuable, individual quality. If you don't accept a shortcoming and battle against it, the shortcoming becomes a flaw. This is exactly how others will perceive it: either as a valuable quality, or as a flaw.

You are perfect, just as Nature and the Creator intended you to be. *Perfection is when an individual is embodying their uniqueness in harmony with their true self.* Where there is acceptance, harmony will appear. And the opposite is true; any negation gives rise to disharmony, which everyone notices.

So, take a good look at your shortcomings, before you hurry to get rid of them. Perhaps, if you accept them, they will transform into your unique qualities and become an advantage? Look attentively, without paying any attention to what other people consider normal! Try to relax at least for a few days and just accept being you. You'll see for yourself what happens. Perhaps, you will end up liking you, just the way you are.

Of course, you still need to be able to distinguish shortcomings from vices. An obvious vice or weak point, that directly harms you, your health and reputation, for example, or that harms others, should be rooted out. Some things are obvious, and there's no need to go into them here.

In everything else, it is better to develop your positive qualities *than to battle with your shortcomings.* Focusing your attention on your shortcomings, including physical ones, that cannot be eliminated, only makes them worse. If, however, you can root out a shortcoming via self-development, then you should work on self-improvement. But only on the condition that you actually have the desire to do so. If you don't desire to change it, then don't trouble yourself and concentrate on your finer qualities. Otherwise, your life will become a constant battle.

Developing existing qualities is much more effective than rooting out your shortcomings, and doing something with them. Developing your finer qualities will, most likely, eclipse your shortcomings or remove them automatically. And then the issue of your shortcomings will fall away of its own accord.

THE THREE ACHIEVEMENTS WAY

You, my little harebrained twits, have no doubt already imagined yourselves as being magnificent? No! I am the magnificent one here! But you can be too if you are audacious enough to let yourself be so! You decide for yourself, the kind of person you want to be. You are more than capable of doing so. And I will teach you how. You will be the happiest and most beautiful of them all. I am Tufti, your priestess! That is the reason I came.

- You occupy the body of a mannequin, as one of your many variations.
- You have to develop, whilst retaining your true self; change, without betraying Self.
- Uniqueness is all you have, and this is enough.
- A shortcoming should either be rooted out or accepted.
- When you accept a personal shortcoming, it can turn into a positive quality.
- Don't battle with your shortcomings, develop your finer qualities.

Before we get into *how to compose your own mannequin*, I'll explain *why this is worth doing* because it's a matter of some importance. Patience, my dears, you will learn all this in good time.

There is one universal formula that is 100% reliable: *life will work out if you accept that you are a unique miracle, with all your shortcomings, just as you are, and then decide to enjoy yourself and the life you have.* If you can simply enjoy life, then you, your life and everything in it will improve automatically.

However, it is quite hard to achieve this. Too great a burden of various moulds and standards, *conventional norms and limitations have been placed on you since birth.* There are three concrete actions you must take in order to free yourself from this burden. One thing is certain, you won't remove this burden with the mind.

First. Don't focus on your shortcomings. *Don't allow yourself to dwell on feeling deprived in some way;* this is a destructive state. The shortcomings will only become worse and this will lead to greater deterioration. You have to shift into a different, more constructive state. This will help with the second action.

Second. You should have a goal in life, something inspiring, that fills you with enthusiasm, and benefits you and others. If you feel apathetic about life in general, then, you don't have a goal. Or, if you look at it from a different perspective, when you have no goal, you feel apathetic about life. When you have no goal, there is nothing to desire. If you experience no sense of striving, there will be no movement in your life. No movement, no energy; no energy, no life. So you must find your true goal, ***your life purpose***, *and begin moving towards it.* Without a life purpose, there is no 'you'; you are simply an empty space. If you haven't yet found a life purpose, the third action will help you to do so.

125

Third. Whether you know what your life purpose is or not, you should concentrate on personal development, *on remaking yourself.* Focus on yourself constantly. Kindle in yourself the Creator's Spark; work on self-development and self-improvement. This method delivers three achievements instantly: first, you shake off any feelings of being deprived; second, you find your life purpose; third, you realise life purpose.

Well, what else did you expect? There is no magic wand. There is the plait though, but you have to work with it. It won't happen whilst you're lying about on the sofa. As you now know, goals are achieved through triple action: propel reality, propel yourself, propel yourself from within. Self-development is always a worthy goal and path. Your life purpose on this path will find itself and once you have found it, there should be no stopping you. Remember: there is either development or deterioration.

You mustn't think of self-development as an onerous duty or heavy chore. Quite the opposite; it's much harder to experience stagnation, inactivity, and laziness. *Working on yourself is no chore but pleasant preparation for something even more pleasurable.* You get ready when you are going to a party, don't you, smartening yourself up? Well, today is the party. A one-time preparation won't be enough for what will come tomorrow, in a month's time or in a year from now.

To summarise what has been said: To become magnificent and turn your life into pure magnificence, you have to shift yourself out of a state of stagnation and degradation. The way out is to find your life purpose, your true goal, and then take steps towards it. Your life purpose is your route to self-realisation. Without a life purpose, life is nothing more than mindless existence. Even if you do not yet know what your life purpose is, the Creator's Spark that smoulders inside you knows. *But the Spark has to be kindled.* By kindling the Creator's Spark and working on yourself, you achieve these three things: you leave stagnation behind; you find your life purpose and you realise your life purpose.

This is why you need to compose a mannequin as well as your reality. Remember the integrated propel-stroll method, and what we said about it? Follow this method, and everything in your life will right itself.

Aside from the issue of your life purpose, there is another good reason to follow this method. Self-development creates movement. I repeat, without movement, there is no energy and without energy, there can be no life, just a fading of life. To trigger meta-power you need to have sufficient amounts of personal power — energy. *When you move, because you are developing yourself, you can receive this energy.*

No one can know better than you, the direction in which you should develop. If you don't have a clear idea yet of what direction you should choose, ask yourself the question and set yourself the goal of developing yourself, and it will come to you.

As far as one's life purpose is concerned, there are other details to be taken into account.

1. Follow the call of the heart. Find the things that are meant for you and the things that could have been made specifically for you, things that are right out of the box.
2. Follow your own path, not the footsteps of others. Don't copy the experience of others. Indulge in the luxury of being unique in everything.

I could write a whole book on this theme. Yes! You will have to read other books aside from this one. Don't be lazy, don't be lazy, my dear ones, but study diligently! You don't want to stay snails forever, do you?

YOU ARE BRILLIANT

Did I say that I didn't like you? I was only joking. You are my favourites, my pets. Don't disappoint me and I won't disappoint you.

- Don't dwell on feeling deprived in some way.
- You must find your true goal, your life purpose and begin moving towards it.
- Your life purpose is what inspires you and benefits others as well as yourself.
- You may not know what your life purpose is, but the Creator's Spark knows; kindle it.
- Self-development helps to shake off stagnation, find your purpose, realise your purpose.
- Without movement and development, you will not have the energy to trigger meta-power.

Do you want to be a better person, improve your physical fitness and appearance, develop skills and talents? Or are you too lazy? What do you mean, you don't want to? Look at yourselves, and the state you are in with your crooked legs, silly horns, round tummies and hungry mouths.

And yet despite all that, you are perfect because the Creator's Spark is present within you. You have to realise your perfection and kindle the Spark. In what manner your perfection will manifest all depends on your personality. Whether it will be revealed at all depends on your intentions.

Let's say you want to have a beautiful body, transform yourself into a charming personality, pleasant in all respects, or become a high-paid professional in a particular field. Essentially, this means occupying your *perfected mannequin on a fundamentally different film roll*. Have no doubt that this film roll and the corresponding mannequin exists. All you have to do is get there. This goal is achieved via triple-action: propel reality, propel yourself, propel yourself from within. Let's look at all three components individually.

1. Propel reality With the help of the plait, compose a reality, in which you already have what you want and already embody the person you want to become. *Compose a new you in a new reality.* Literally, do this several times during the day or more. Become fully present, activate the plait, and without losing a sense of the plait, picture the scene you desire (the end result, the target frame) with your thoughts and words; visualise it as best you can. Do the exercise in a relaxed manner for no more than a minute at a time. Remember that it is concentration and meta-power that makes this technique work, not effort and force.

Don't hold back when you set your goal. Go for it! Think big and set your sights high from the outset. Set yourself a goal that will awaken the genius in you; become a genius in a specific field or in your general attitude towards life. Then, *regardless of your specific abilities, you will start being brilliant.*

That said, if you have no aptitude at all for something that attracts you, it might be worth considering whether this is, in fact, your true path. But if you are following your heart's desire and if your goal is basically achievable, then there is no

129

reason why it should not be realised; beyond that, it all comes down to perseverance and composing a new you in a new reality consistently and coherently. Remember you have the Spark of the Creator within, which you can kindle into a flame and turn into a masterpiece.

After some time, you will see that you are beginning to do things you couldn't do before and that you probably were not even capable of doing. This will surprise you and yet there is nothing superhuman about it. *It is no miracle, just a technique.* By setting a reality, in which you are brilliant, you move onto film rolls, in which you do brilliant things; I repeat, the reason for this is *not that you have the necessary abilities per se, but because that is the nature of the script.*

It simply comes down to the fact that on other film rolls, you will have things that you don't have currently and haven't even considered. There, in a new mannequin, new abilities will manifest themselves and new means of realising your ideas can be found. You will spot them, as long as you aren't sleeping.

2. ***Propel yourself*** I remind you that to propel yourself in relation to other people means to compose an image. To propel yourself in relation to the reality of your everyday life means to compose a reflection. In a general sense, the act of propelling involves being consciously aware of your motives and actions.

When you aren't consciously aware, and are just drifting in accordance with the script, all the messages you put out to the mirror that concern other people will be reduced to "give me-give me-give me", and those that concern reality will come down to, 'I want, I want, I want'. And yet, there comes a point in time, when you are able to release yourself from the script. Then you can become fully present and recall the image composition method and the reflection composition method.

In relation to other people, replace all your 'give me's' with 'here, take!'. After persistent practice, this manner will become a habit and start to create an impression. You'll naturally become a very charming personality without having to fake it because your habits make up part of your mannequin. Together with your own transformation, you'll see that the problems that troubled you so much have either solved themselves or simply fallen away. Take a good look at the 'Setting An Image' chapter and there you'll see all the 'give me's' and the corresponding 'here, take' alternatives.

The same thing goes for reality: whatever happens, you have the method for composing a goal frame, the principles of use, as well as the allowing and following methods. Remember also that all negative thoughts and messages will return to haunt you like a boomerang. Try and turn all the negative signs into plus signs for your own benefit, and then this too will become a habit that makes up part of your new mannequin.

What should you do if, right now, you can't think of anything that you can give or any message you want to put out to the universe? This is where the imitation technique comes in handy. *You can transform the reflection into an image or subject by pretending that you already have something you do not currently have, or that you already are the person you would like to be but have not yet become. As the game, so the reality; what you imitate is what you get; who you fake is who you will become.* The reflection flows into an image. We will go into this in more detail in the next chapter.

THE IMITATION TECHNIQUE

You are probably beginning to think, dear ones, that with all these methods, you could end up being a clockwork mannequin? Don't worry, my little fidgets; it is better to be a wind-up mannequin with good habits than a puppet of no sound mind.

- New mannequins are created via triple action: propel reality, propel yourself, propel from within.
- Use the plait to compose a new you in a new reality.
- Think big, but make sure your goals are realistic.
- Soon, you'll be doing things that you didn't previously think yourself capable of doing.
- New abilities appear and develop on new film rolls.
- The ways and means of realising your idea will automatically present themselves.
- It can be helpful to repeat the chapters that explain what it means to 'propel yourself'.

At the end of our last lesson, we said that the imitation technique will enable you to acquire qualities that you don't yet have. Let's recall the objectives we set: acquire a beautiful body, transform yourself into a charming personality, pleasant in all regards, and become a highly paid professional. Even though you might not yet have all this right now, you can fake having it right now. Then, as you already know, reality will find a way of manifesting the illusion you have created on the physical plane.

You should literally imagine that you already have all these positive things despite the fact that, so far at least, you're faking it and it is just a game. Observe other people, who have these things. Initially, copy how they hold themselves, especially if you don't have your own image of what this might look like. For your draft version, the experience of others will do. Later, your individuality will begin to show itself more strongly.

Take note of what you admire in other people. Irrespective of whether they work in the same field as you. You can always learn from brilliance. I do such and such just as brilliantly as so and so does. Is there something you admire? I want to be able to do the same, and can create the same wonderful life for myself. Soak up the finesse that you find so attractive and adapt it to your life, as a projection. Declare this intention using the plait. You only need to capture a projection of brilliance rather than trying to copy it in every detail. What is essential is the projection, not the specific form it takes.

I want to emphasise, that you don't need to copy an entire example, just the person's state, *their sense of self and general air*. Adopt a state that makes you feel good about yourself: you have a beautiful body; you have a charming personality; you are a highly paid professional. How would you feel if this were the case? What you would feel is the required state you must capture for this exercise. What you have determined the emotional state, behave as if you already had what you are striving for.

Create a virtual reality with your thoughts. Illuminate that visualisation with the plait from time to time. Recall your vi-

133

sion more frequently; run it in the background, be consistent. Even if your physical body and everything else about you is far from being perfect, you can still *live the feeling; fake it; become accustomed to it*.

Is this copying? Yes, it is out and out copying, but if your approach is serious and consistent, reality will take it very seriously indeed. Reality will not tolerate an illusion that is not of its own making so the illusions that you create will either be manifest in the physical plane or destroyed. Don't worry, my darlings, the latter is highly unlikely, as long as you don't go looking for trouble or push things too far. Even children know that a game is a game and keep within the limits of what is real.

You will easily sense the limits of reality in your own game. Playing the role of a charming personality is totally within your capacity especially when you are equipped with the image composition method. You naturally won't be able to take the stage at a ballet or walk out onto a hockey pitch and behave like a professional if you've never done it before, because you have not yet reached the necessary film roll. However, your imitation game will be no less effective because of it. All in good time. This is what the third action is for.

3. *Propel yourself* It is important to be realistic and understand that sofa metaphysics alone are not enough. We live in a dual world, so you have to take action equivalent to the material plane. Do everything you can to achieve your goal within the current frame, and shape your new self. You need to improve yourself not only with the help of the plait, but also physically, by means of concrete exercises, study, steps to improve your diet and lifestyle. There is nothing you can do to change this requirement.

Once you embark on the path of self-improvement, you will know what to do and how. The information will find its way to you. It is also particularly important to be aware that on the path of self-development, your life purpose will be revealed to you. You can puzzle over questions such as, what your life purpose is, what it will involve, and how to find it as much as you like, but once you set the goal to propel yourself rather than be directed entirely by the script, the answers to all these questions will appear organically.

There is no need to worry about the ways and means of realising your life purpose either. You can't imagine what the ways and means will be because they lie on other film rolls that you still need to reach. There is no doubt that you will reach them if you initiate all three types of action. You have a huge advantage because your competitors usually only use one type of action, the third. Many put a huge amount of effort into this but to no great effect.

Which works most effectively, the first, second or third action? It all depends. On average, they are all roughly equally effective, but if you integrate all three rather than practicing them individually, the results are one hundred percent guaranteed. In any case, the triple action rights the course your reality is taking and things sort themselves out in all areas of your life.

How much time will it take? The answer is forever because, as you know, in life there is always either development or deterioration.

THOUGHT FORMS

You, my boring ones, probably don't quite understand what the difference is between composing a new reality and composing a new self. For in both cases, you compose new film rolls and new mannequins. You will understand soon though.

- Take note of what you admire in other people.
- Adopt their general state and sense of self as a projection.
- In this state, behave as you would as if you already had what you strive for.
- Live in this state, live the feeling, grow accustomed to it.
- Along with the metaphysical work, create yourself on the physical plane too.
- Do whatever is required to achieve your goal in the current frame.
- Once on the path of self-development, the answers to all your questions will come to you.

By composing an image of a new reality, you illuminate the forthcoming frame. Here reality works like a film roll. By imitating an example of your new mannequin, you compose a reflection, which then flows into an image of the subject. In this case, reality works like a mirror. Both the image composition and the imitation process should be carried out using the plait.

Only reality should be composed purposefully, by setting aside special time, several times a day, although without letting it become a burden. In imitation, you live it. Fake it, play with it, feel your way into your new role at the same time as taking a serious approach and being consistent. It does not matter too much if you forget sometimes about the plait; the most important thing is that you live the role, just as actors do prior to a fi lm shoot.

When you're doing this, be open to allow in information concerning your new mannequin and new reality and try yourself out in this new role, as far as circumstances will allow, as well as in your thoughts and visualisations. You may find certain types of mental construct supportive, i.e. thought forms, which you should repeat to yourself as often as possible. For example,

< I am a high ranking specialist unique in my field. My services are in great demand. I derive much pleasure from my work. My contribution is highly valued. I do everything brilliantly. >

< I don't go out to work. I focus on the home, the family, and the children. As a wife and mother, I am one in a million. My husband is in love with me. The children adore me. I also love them all and take care of them. The atmosphere in our home is cosy and joyful. I cheer everyone up. >

< I am in perfect health. I have a strong, toned, sexy body. It doesn't matter how old I am. I have the body of a twenty year old and I always will have. I will always be twenty because that is what I have decided. I feel amazing. I have high levels of vitality and a powerful energy field. >

< I am a very charming individual. There is a certain metaphysical glow about me. People sense it and are drawn to me.

I have my own individual charm. I am generally a very attractive (charismatic) person. Everyone enjoys my company. I bring with me a feeling of joy and celebration. People are drawn to me. Everyone likes me. >

You can write thought forms like this to suit your taste and mood. Activate the plait and say them aloud or to yourself, it doesn't matter which. At the same time, try to behave in a way that correlates to the affirmations, even though you are still aware that it is a game, albeit a serious one. At the same time, work on yourself, and achieve conformity with your vision on the physical plane. Total success is achieved via triple action.

Qualities like charm, wit, intelligence, confidence, and genius, are relatively easy to manifest with just the first two types of action. When it comes to physical attributes, things are a little more complicated. Here you have to focus on the third type of action.

It is worth remembering that physical attractiveness largely depends on the inner qualities, which you consider shortcomings that gnaw away at you. Inferiority complexes leave a very noticeable imprint on a person's face and figure. With the acquisition of certain virtues, the complex will fall way and you will change so much that people will stop recognising you.

Even in the case of physical limitations, the body of your mannequin can be significantly improved. Or rather, it will become a different mannequin, which you need to occupy. Everything is possible with due perseverance, including reversing the ageing process.

Certain physical qualities are built into your DNA but far from everything. DNA cannot hold so much information that it defines all the subtle details of your portrait. Your DNA only determines your main characteristics, those that determine whether you are a human being or a snail, as well as the basic qualities that distinguish you from others like you. It would be more accurate to say that, the information contained within your DNA is barely enough to describe your embryo.

So where is all the rest? For official science, the rest remains a mystery as mainstream science does not want to accept the existence of the information space, which we call the Eternity archive. There is much that science cannot embrace because it has taken upon itself the heavy responsibility of explaining everything from a 'scientific' point of view. And what science is incapable of explaining it either negates or ignores. However, things unexplained do not cease to exist.

So, a significant portion of the information for your "design" is contained in that very information space. And you can correct the design in question. You will learn how to do this, my dears.

THOUGHT MARKERS

Admit it, you envy me for being so marvellous and incomparable, while you are absurd and awkward! You may envy me, but I won't allow you to envy others. Work on yourself!

- By setting yourself a new reality, you use an aspect of the film roll.
- Imitating a new mannequin, you use an aspect of the mirror.
- In both cases, activate the plait and declare your thought forms.
- Let new information in and start living your new role.
- At the same time, work on yourself, and conform to your vision on the physical plane.
- Physical attributes can be significantly improved via triple action.

Before explaining how to correct the design according to which you developed after undergoing the embryonic stage, we will digress slightly. As far as I remember, I called you to invent your own thought forms, according to your own taste and mood. In truth, your mind is not capable of inventing anything new, that is, literally construct something new totally independently. It can only read information, *by managing its awareness*. Have you forgotten who you are? You are film characters!

The brain has three main functions: The first two involve perceiving your environment and interpreting it. The third is less well known and involves the settings, settings for the memory, *one's thinking and condition*. The brain does not generate thoughts or store memories. It works similarly to a radio or a TV set. When you remember something, the brain attunes to an information block situated in the Eternity archive. When you think about something, it also attunes, scans the information and in this way creates from it a flow, which manifests as a train of thought. Thoughts and memories are not stored inside the brain, they are stored outside of the brain, where you would expect information to be, in the information space.

Condition is something slightly more interesting still. This is the feeling you have of yourself, as you were when you were created by Nature, or rather, in accordance with the design. If you reconcile yourself to the fact and accept whatever has been given you by Nature, then this is how you will remain. Alternatively, you can change, for the better or for worse. Here, both the course of your strivings and society have an impact.

Depending on personal characteristics and life circumstances, you may either consider yourself to be a good-looking, fortunate soul or an ugly loser. This is what is meant by your condition. Whenever your sense of self is aligned with one feeling or the other, your condition synchronises with the design. And if there is a mismatch, the design corrects itself, one way or the other. So, regardless of the initial parameters of the design, you can turn from a darling of lady luck into a very unsympathetic brat, or, the opposite, transform from an ugly duckling into an all-round favourite.

Now here's a question: Is it possible to control the synchronisation process? You probably already know the answer to that.

The characters who lack awareness drift along with the script, relying on a random 'it'll either work out or it won't', 'I'll be lucky or I won't', helplessly floundering in the current frame. In this case, synchronisation occurs automatically, unprompted by the character. And then, the lucky one becomes a star, and the one whom things didn't work out for slips down a slippery slope into a hole.

You, my favourites, not only create your own, new reality, you create yourself anew, remake yourself, attuning to the new you, which means that you intentionally acquire a new condition.

But this is not the same thing as synchronisation. In the moment you declare your thought form you compose a new reality, which has not yet become manifest. Even practising the imitation technique, you still don't fully enter into the necessary condition. So what happens next? Next, you shift onto new film rolls, occupy new mannequins and see real progress with your own eyes. You will undoubtedly see progress and then you will say to yourself, 'this does actually work!' And then, you will genuinely acquire a new state of being.

When you achieve this new state of being, your thought forms will be transformed into thought markers.

 # It turns out that I compose my own reality. #
 # My intention really works. #
 # I really am occupying a new mannequin. #

Thought markers state that such and such a thing is actually happening. The statement of it confirms the thing as fact. Unlike thought forms, thought markers serve as bookmarks — descriptions of something that has already happened and no longer requires proof.

Thought forms, on the other hand, are affirmations that strive to prove their validity. The desire to prove something to

142

yourself or others is always unconvincing. Whether you wish to convince yourself or reality, both attempts are ineffective. You can pretend, but you won't ever be able to convince yourself of something that has not yet happened in physical reality. Positive affirmations will never carry you into a pure condition that exists beyond a shred of doubt. The only thing that is totally effective is confirmation. Thought markers refer to things that are already confirmed.

Of course, thought forms as affirmations also have an impact on the design, but a weaker impact, because synchronisation only occurs in the moment that you come face to face with the reality of a situation as fact. Thought forms are effective at the initial stage, when a new reality is being launched. Then, when you start to see the first results and your progress, pay special attention to them and again, use the plait and state that your efforts really are working.

In this moment, you come into contact with outer intention and, in this moment, synchronisation occurs with the design. *Thought forms compose reality; thought markers adjust the design.* So, carry out all three types of action, observe the shifts and then consolidate them with thought markers:

Every day, I get closer to achieving my goal.
I really do manage everything brilliantly. My level of professionalism is growing.
I really am getting physically fitter.
I really am becoming a more charming and attractive person.

GREEDY CATCHERS

The theme of the previous lesson was quite complicated. Would you like to consolidate what we covered? What do you mean, you don't want to?! Come on, crawl out of your houses! Everyone, horns up! Or you will be punished.

- The mind does not invent anything; it reads information from the Eternity archive.
- There are three main functions of the brain: perception, interpretation, setting.
- The brain works as a receiver, attuning to memory, thought and condition.
- Condition refers to your sense of self, as you really are, in all your subtle details.
- Condition does not refer to changing moods; it refers to your sense of self.
- The design, similarly to your condition, can change for the better or the worse.
- In moments of awareness, your condition synchronises with the design.

- Regardless of the initial design, you can take off and fly or slide down a slippery slope.
- Carrying out the triple action, you shift yourself into a new condition.
- Imitation becomes genuine when you observe results.
- Thought markers confirm that improvements are taking place.
- Thought forms trigger a new reality; thought markers adjust the design.

Do you remember I mentioned previously that, when you practise the imitation technique, you create an illusion for reality? I'll repeat this point now. If there is something you want, pretend that you already have it. If there is someone you want to become, behave as if you were already that person. Be in the role, take it seriously and live it *like a professional actor*. Live it in your thoughts, in virtual space, and where possible, in your actions, in your everyday reality, until you totally believe in the illusion you have created. As soon as you believe in it, reality will believe in it too.

When will you believe it? When you see a tangible proof that the technique really works. This is why I so strongly recommend that you always pay special attention to any shifts you notice taking place. As soon as you spot a change, immediately activate the plait and savour your achievements, taking pleasure in all the details.

And then, how does the miracle happen? Your design is adjusted! You become a little (or perhaps very) different. It is the same as if you were occupying a new body in a new outfit. If you regularly perform all three actions, you will gradually shift to ever higher levels.

And now for the method, my little boring ones; Again and again! ***The synchronisation method.***

1. Carry out all three actions, either separately or simultaneously, whichever you prefer.
2. Observe carefully and avidly grasp any confirmation of your success.
3. As soon as you see a sign of success, activate the plait and consolidate the shift with a thought marker.

Positive shifts will occur both in the context of the manifestation of your vision, as well as in relation to the means by which it is being realised. Reality will throw your potential means of realising your vision and encourage you to use them.

There will also be moments of 'defeat'. These are unavoidable. What matters is how you respond to them. When you suffer defeat, your condition changes and you feel a failure. And what happens to the design in this moment? I hate to think. On no account must you let this type of synchronisation occur! So, how do you avoid it?

It is very simple. Surely you haven't forgotten the wonderful principle you have at your disposal? Advantage! You probably haven't yet eradicated your stupid habit of insisting on your own script. Well, hang on in there, otherwise I'll eradicate you myself! Or better still, I'll immortalise you in jars of formaldehyde and show you off to my other students, not for self-edification you understand, but for inspiration! They will become instantly more clever and obedient.

And on the other hand, if you have been lucky enough to secure a victory, nurture and savour your condition carefully, not forgetting the plait. Have no doubt, your design will adjust itself and things will develop in a more positive manner. You must be very attentive and responsible when it comes to your condition; *manage it.*

And also, I remember saying, that if you set the right goal, the script might even shock you. You might feel that your life

146

is falling apart at the seams, whereas in actual fact, old 'stuff' is being cleared from your reality so that the empty space can be filled with beautiful new things.

And anyway, how can you know by what means your goal should best be realised? It might seem to you as if nothing is going right, whereas in fact, everything is going perfectly, just not in the way you planned it. And anyway, who ever promised that your path would be strewn with roses?

And you mustn't let the fact that you aren't seeing instant results worry you either. Take into account the fact that reality responds with a delay factor. Be patient, be persistent and consistent. If nothing is working out at all and you feel as if you are knocking at a door that will never open, then you should ask yourself whether this really is your true path and the path of your heart's desire. The only path, that will never let you down is the path of self-development. Not any path, of course, (such as studying ancient Greek), but the path that will inspire you and bear real fruit.

And one more thing: *You can only compose your new self by using the reality mirror* and the plait. Don't try and compose your new mannequin while looking in a normal mirror. I forbid you to try it! It either won't work, or it will have the opposite effect. *When you stand in front of a flat mirror, you can only note positive developments while ignoring your shortcomings.* You mustn't focus your attention on the shortcomings you'd like to be shot of. *Shortcomings should be either eradicated through self-improvement or accepted as an aspect of your individuality.* If you can't do anything about them, then, let them be.

147

SWEET HARMONY

Yes, yes, I know, I know, when it comes to laudatory, captivating speeches addressed to my highest self, you lot are churlish, indeed most churlish misers, and of my success, you are greedy, indeed most greedy scrooges. And so you are! But not to worry, I shan't be in your debt; I will store a bitter grudge against you and, when I have saved up enough, I shall settle the score.

- Pay special attention to positive shifts.
- The design is adjusted in the moment you consolidate the shift with a thought marker.
- Greedily catch hold of any confirmation of your success, savour them, enjoy them.
- Confirmation of results will carry you into a pure condition.
- Regular, systematic practice of the three actions will perfect your design.
- You mustn't look at failure and see failure, or look at defeat and see defeat.
- The path of self-development is the only path that will never let you down.
- Either you manage your condition, or your condition manages you.

This final point is extremely important. I hope you understand the significance of the meaning. You must be very attentive and responsible when it comes to your condition; manage it because, firstly, it is the key to your design, and secondly, there is something else, of which we shall speak now.

Just because you have woken up in a film doesn't make you invulnerable. Because you are in a film, anything that happens in the film can also happen to you. You awakening does not change the film. Your task is to create a film in which everything works out favourably for you. If, however, something unfavourable does happen, you still have one failsafe fallback principle — Advantage.

In addition to applying the advantage method to situations that have already taken place, you can also create advantage from events that have not yet occurred. I will not bore you now with yet another method; the principle here is simple: *if it works out then great, and if it doesn't, even better*. This applies to events that are so important to you that the very importance you attribute to them hinders their smooth, successful implementation, such that even the plait cannot rescue you. And since this is the case, declare beforehand that whatever outcome the event may have, it will be advantageous to you and therefore successful. This reduces the intensity of the importance you attribute to the event and it will also lift your mood. Anyway, you don't really know, do you, exactly what turn of events in the script will work in your favour. We have already discussed this before.

Although constantly composing a film roll, in which everything turns out favourably for you, is a beneficial habit, sometimes it can feel tiring and a bit full-on. So, what does this mean? You can't ever relax now? You can, you can!

Along with all of the principles we have covered thus far, there is another aspect of reality worth considering: 'the weather at home', or, in other words, the atmosphere of the current filmstrip. We are not talking about the weather as such, rather the general condition of reality, which may be aggressive, or harmonious, and which is personal to you because everyone else is living in relatively different conditions. Everyone has their own 'weather'. For example, in one and the same geographical area, you may have a blue lagoon, while someone else has an icy desert.

So, the weather in your current reality is determined by your condition. By condition here, we mean not only the type of condition we talked about very recently but your state of mind and mood as well as your attitude to everything around you.

Both your condition in particular and the condition of your reality can be expressed in one general term: *sweet harmony*. The sweetness in this term is nothing to do with marmalade. Obviously this word in particular has many meanings. Above all the term refers to harmony, in the sense that all shall be well. It also refers to pleasure and delight — the sweet life. To get along sweetly means to live in peace and harmony. Sweet harmony is when the world is at peace, there is order and prosperity in your life, and all is well. 'Sweet' can also mean 'my sweet' or 'my love'. If you love life, life will overflow with sweet harmony. If you love yourself, life will be filled with delight. And if you don't love yourself, create harmony and you will begin to love yourself.

Do you remember the law? If you allow yourself to be guided by the principle of Advantage, there will be fewer and fewer events in your life that are in some way harmful. There will be harmony, but life is even better if you can create sweet harmony intentionally, i.e. attune yourself to a corresponding state.

There was a reason why I advised you to copy the general air and sense of self of the people you look to as role models. This is not only the key to your perfect design, but also the things that create attraction. What is it about your role models

150

that attracts you? No doubt a very positive manner that life is good, success, style, beauty, charm, and pleasure. *Pleasure is the first* thing that people seek. People are drawn to those who radiate happiness and, by and large, they are all drawn to sweet harmony!

And what else is drawn to sweet harmony? Reality! Reality loves sweet harmony too and becomes harmonious around people and for people who radiate the same. Dissatisfaction, irritation, hostility and similar attitudes do the exact opposite: they repel others and they make reality frown.

What should we conclude from this? Try and maintain a condition of sweet harmony. Look for pleasure in small things and there, you will find it. Use any excuse to create a special occasion and life will be one continual celebration. Create a light, sunny atmosphere both within yourself and around you. Merely expressing a benevolent attitude towards others is enough to evoke their good will towards you. And a benevolent attitude towards your reality, whatever the circumstances, will evoke the good will of reality itself. *Deliberately create a positive atmosphere.* Make this a habit. This is probably the most beneficial habit of all those we have covered.

Radiating happiness, love, comfort, and joy, more specifically, sweet harmony, you attract people and a successful reality also. For everyone wants the same thing. *People are drawn to those with good fortune, those who know how to create the sweet life. You look at the screens and the magazine covers and you see people who are super successful, comfortable, beautiful and happy — it's enough to make you sick — and you think when you compare yourself to them, that your life has not worked out as it should.* But believe me, all that showy beauty and happiness is, for the large part, all down to props and bluffs. What's more, now you know how to create real, genuine sweet harmony. And, most importantly, you are capable of doing so. All right? Am I right? Of course, I'm right. For I am Tufti, your priestess!

PLAIT WITH THREADS

So, my gracious ones, I hope you have understood that sweet harmony is when all is well, and as it should be. Sweet harmony occurs not only when everything is truly well and as it should be but when you deliberately adopt a state of sweet harmony whatever is going on, and then, all is well indeed. It is like having the ability to change the weather.

- Set the advantage in advance: *if it works out, great, if it doesn't, even better.*
- The weather in your current reality depends directly on your condition.
- Sweet harmony means fun, comfort, love, friendliness, and celebration.
- People are drawn to fortunate others, who know how to radiate sweet harmony.
- Reality becomes supportive to those who radiate sweet harmony.
- Stay in control of your own state of mind; do not just let it free-run.

Letting your state of mind free-run is paramount to hanging like a cloth puppet in someone else's hands and dangling about to the will of chance or the will of another. Create your own personal Sweet harmony. *Bring light into any company.* Create your own oasis in the frame, the oasis of a happy, celebratory mood. My oasis comes with me: wherever I am, my oasis is there with me. Begin the day with the words 'Sweet harmony'. Always make a point of getting into this state, whatever the circumstances. Just Sweet harmony, that's all.

If you are feeling annoyed or overcome with fear or anger, don't fight the emotions, just begin observing. Anything amiss that is happening should nudge you to observe what is going on in your life and your reality. When you look at fear under a magnifying glass, paradoxically, it gets smaller. When you observe reality, it loses its power. Reality doesn't like being watched. It becomes elusive and, at the same time, ceases to have so much control over you. Don't stare at reality, *just take a sideways glance, so that it does not get annoyed at you.*

Finally, I want to give you a bit more detail about the plait. Firstly, don't be too perplexed if you can't feel the plait or only get a very vague sense of it. All these sensations are very personal — that's quite normal. For example, my friend Matilda does not sense a plait but rather a slight feeling of oppression from behind, a kind of presence of something non-corporeal *and phantom-like.*

This sense of presence can manifest itself in different ways. It might be something you can actually feel, but if you have to imagine it, that's fine too. Imagine that someone has attached a hard, straight plait to the back of your head. You shake your head, feel that the plait is there, and then remove it. Although the plait is no longer there, the sense that it was there a moment ago remains with you. This is what is described as a phantom sensation.

If the phantom feeling doesn't work for you, it's not a problem; try the following technique instead. Imagine that an arrow or compass needle is hanging down from the nape of your neck to the middle of your back. Then, take an in-breath, and when you exhale, imagine that the arrow has turned so that it is now at an angle to your back. If you experience the phantom sensation, you can use this technique to activate the plait.

It doesn't matter what angle the arrow is exactly or how much distance there is between the arrow and your spine. Your energy body will tell you how far the arrow should be from your back for it to become active. Even if you activate the plait without the arrow, simply focus your attention on a certain spot at roughly an elbow's distance or less from the middle of your shoulders, and that should be enough. With time, after a certain amount of practice, you will learn to feel the plait quite tangibly. The plait also needs training: it has atrophied from lack of use.

And now for another technique for advanced snails, that makes the plait even more effective. Imagine that a flow of energy is rising up along the central axis of your body. Take an in-breath and observe a certain sensation rising from your feet up to your head. Next, imagine the reverse flow, from the top down. Exhale and track the downward sensation. Practice this several times. On the in-breath the flow rises upwards; on the out-breath the flow moves downwards. The sensations may be phantom-like, but the energy flow is absolutely real, it's just that until you really practice you may not be aware of it.

Now imagine, that two arrows protrude from your chest in opposite directions: from the chest (or from the stomach) outwards and from between the shoulders (or lower) and backwards. Take an in-breath and then on the out-breath, imagine that the arrow in front is turning into an upward vertical position and the arrow behind you is turning in a vertical position pointing downwards. Try to sense both energy currents as they flow simultaneously. The rising current, triggered by the fron-

154

tal arrow, moves along the whole body just a little forward of the central axis, while the descending current triggered by the arrow behind the back also flows along the length of the whole body slightly beyond the axis. Or simply imagine that they both move simultaneously, one upwards and the other downwards, without any specific 'positioning', depending on which is easiest for you to feel.

Repeat this exercise several times, so that you really start to feel the energy flow in the body. Then, on an out-breath try and trigger both energy flows at the same time, without picturing the arrows. Then activate the plait, like you did using arrow from the nape of the neck, breathe a little, and then on the out-breath, move it sharply downwards into a vertical position, at the same time triggering both energy currents. You should get the hang of it after just a little practice.

Again, just as you work with the plait without tension, do the same with the currents. You just trigger the energy flow, but it moves of its own accord. Simply get the energy going and then let the flow continue moving through the body of its own accord.

And now, ***the plait and flow method***.
1. Take an in-breath, and on the out-breath imagine the arrow moving at an angle away from your back. Now the plait is activated.
2. Without letting go of the sensation of the plait, compose a picture of your reality. At the same time, make sure that you are breathing freely.
3. Without losing the sense of the plait (the arrow), take an in-breath and on the out-breath sharply send the arrow into a vertical downward position, triggering both energy flows.
4. Staying aware of the movement of the rising and descending energy flows, say the following thought form quietly to yourself or aloud: My intention is being realised.

155

5. Then let go of all the sensations you have been working with.

What is happening when you do this? You are not only composing your own reality with the help of the plait, you are putting out (sending) your intention as a 'message' to the universe. In this way, the energy flow strengthens the work of the plait. If this technique works for you and you enjoy it, you can use this variation of the exercise all the time. But if not, then the basic method will be sufficient.

Another effective way of using the plait is to work with it whilst you are in the bath or any other source of water. For example, make the most of the time that you are in the bath. Activate the plait (the walls of the bath hinder the exercise) without the energy currents, and compose a picture of your own reality and/or yourself — your new mannequin. You don't have to try too hard. It is enough to concentrate for two or three minutes in total and then drop the plait and then just relax in the bath for another ten minutes.

What is the point of this? In this case, the plait is working as well as the water, which, as we know, is readily charged with the information content of your thought forms (as well as thought markers, obviously). The water does not send your intention out into the universe. In this case, its function is different. First, the water absorbs the information you are giving it, then it literally 'imprints' your subtle (energy) body with the same information. Water is highly effective in fulfilling this function. When you are immersed in water, you can be totally charged, (imprinted) with your intention, and then you walk around like a living radio station, broadcasting it throughout the atmosphere.

If you don't have a bath, there is another option you can use — the contrast shower. At first, spend a couple of minutes warming up in hot (not too hot) water, and turn on the cold water for no more than five minutes. Repeat the same three or four times. The greater the contrast in temperatures the better, but more important than that, you shouldn't experience extreme discomfort and damage your health.

Postpone working with the plait when doing this procedure because it will be harder to concentrate than when you are in the bath. A contrast shower, however, dramatically increases your energy flow, so for this reason, when you turn off the water, be calm, focus and then practise the plait and flow method. This is also a very effective technique.

That's it. It's all very simple. The plait isn't a gadget that you can or can't afford to purchase — you already have it, and you always will. And, of course, no super-gadget can give you what the plait will. Nonetheless, use it intentionally and purposefully; don't 'chat' with it unnecessarily.

THE POWER OF PAST INCARNATIONS

So, then, my darlings! We won't consolidate what we have covered any more. For you, from now on, repetition will take the form of re-reading this book, perhaps, more than once because even having carried out the recommended practices, you couldn't have understood or remembered everything first time round, and all the more so if you didn't actually try out the techniques while you were reading the book. I have been there. I know.

With each new reading you will surprise yourself as you discover something new, as if you were reading the book for the first time. Try to reread this material at least once and discover this for yourself.

The last thing I want to tell you is something of which you won't suspect, like for example, you were not aware of the existence of the plait — your birthright. As you now know, you have the right to compose your forthcoming reality and even a new mannequin, but there is something more. You have the right to personal power, accumulated over the course of your past life incarnations.

What is the meaning of life in principle? *Life itself.* Only this and aside from this, there is no other 'deep' philosophical meaning. What is the meaning of the existence of the planet or a single grain of sand? There is none. They simply are – that's all. There is no fundamental difference between the meaning of the existence of the living and the non-living. The meaning lies simply in that all these things *are*, and glory be to the Creator.

So what is the meaning of successive incarnations? The answer is also nothing, well, almost nothing. Every subsequent life, from the birth and death of a butterfly, to the birth and death of the universe, is the dream of the Creator, whose Spark is present in all things. In the same way, every one of your lives is nothing more than the dream of the Creator, tantamount to your own dream of course.

Why all this should be, can only be known to the Creator. So what can be known to us? We ought to know what we are capable of and what we are entitled to. This knowledge, however, is not given to all, only to those who seek it. If you have no desire to know anything about these things, then live however you see fit. The meaning of life is in life itself, and life is enough.

The value just as the meaning of all things in existence is equal. Your life is no more valuable than the life of a snail which you might squash underfoot without even noticing.

Of course, I was exaggerating when I called you snails and freaks but not without good reason. The question is, whether what you know and what you have been given is enough for you. If it is enough, then that is all well and good. Everyone has the right to live their life without questioning things. None could blame a snail for living as a normal, non-conscious being because a snail is non-conscious by its very nature. But is it blameless (and can it really be laudable) to live like a non-conscious character when one is endowed with the capacity for self-awareness? That is the question.

Of course, none of that refers to you, my dear ones. Since you are already reading this book, you are one of those people who are not satisfied with what is commonly known and what has been given to you. You cannot imagine what prominent, and perhaps, even great people you once were, in your previous incarnations. Undoubtedly you were great, otherwise you would not have earned this life.

But, regardless of any former greatness, all that now has been wasted and lost. You do not remember your former incarnations. Do you not think that strange? Again, one might ask the question: what is the point of these past lives? There were failures and defeats, victories and achievements. You have paid for much and accomplished much. Has all that really been for nothing, simply in vain?

You cannot bring back the experience of forgotten lives, just as you cannot take with you something you possessed in a forgotten dream. Still, I repeat, *you have a right to the personal power accumulated over the course of numerous incarnations*. No-one has told you this before, **but I** am telling you now.

Personal power and strength of soul should not be wasted. A new life should never begin entirely from scratch. That would be a mistake, a glitch in creation. Whether you accept it and live with the mistake is a matter of will. Only what good are you to anyone as a defective being? You are no good even to me. It is within your power to claim what is rightfully yours, but *how*?

It is very simple. Anyone who declares their right is given it. You literally need to say: **I declare my right. I return my power. I acquire the power of all my previous incarnations.**

Words, however, are not enough. Words are so often empty talk. There is one subtle detail here. For your words to be heard, you have to use that archaic rudiment of which you are already aware: the plait.

Make your declaration using the plait just as you did when you were composing your own reality and Power will hear you. Do this, whenever you feel it is necessary. You will soon gradually come to sense an increase in your personal power, *self-confidence ,and strength of spirit.* You will definitely feel it and every time you do feel confirmation that it is working, do not forget to consolidate your renewed design with thought markers such as: # *I can see that my personal power really is increasing.* #

There is nothing more to add here. You will see for yourself how amazing it is.

INFINITY IN INFINITY

And now, we will talk about something which many an inquisitive mind will sceptically await: proof, proof that everything we have talked about here is real. @ Surely we don't really live in a film? And surely we can't jump from one film roll to another? @

Well, first of all, the main proof should lie in your own empirical experience. The methods and techniques described here really work; check it out for yourself. And secondly, much indirect proof, particularly indirect proof, can be found in the form of anomalous and unexplained phenomena. You won't find direct proof that these techniques work because, for some reason, reality is not prone to revealing its secrets.

How is it, you may be wondering, that I know all about these methods? There is much I do not know. What I do know is that this stuff works and that's a fact. Why and how exactly is another question. Film rolls and the mirror are just models and interpretations of something more complex. We may not understand how exactly reality works, but we can and should use the qualities of reality for our own practical purposes. And so for this reason, I put forward these models and interpretations that are accessible to our understanding. There is one thing I can confidently confirm: *if the model works then it must be very close to the original.*

Therefore, we will stick to the accepted model. Reality is live, not virtual. Don't confuse it with a computer game. But it is constructed similarly to a film, or more precisely, numerous film rolls that are all intertwined. Some of these film rolls are moving, while others are still in the archive.

Parallel *material* worlds don't exist. There is only one material universe (in any case, the one that is ours), but there are countless virtual variations of the world — the archive film rolls. It sometimes happens that a piece of one archival filmstrip is randomly illuminated in the current (material) frame. In this case, a person from the past, the future, or another civilisation entirely, could end up here in the present.

When a person ends up here, in our world, from the archive, their last life will seem very real to them because their memory is so tied to the film roll from whence they came. *The brain does not store information. It stores the information's address.* When moving from one film roll to another, addresses can become detached from the former film roll and become attached to the new one, although this is not always the case. This accounts for the déjà vu effect.

The déjà vu effect is when you are certain that something has already happened in your life, but everyone around you insists that it has not. Or the opposite, people tell you that something happened, but you can't for the life of you remember it, not because you are having a memory glitch, but because there is confusion between the addresses and the film rolls. Reality does sometimes make mistakes like these.

Although reality does try very carefully to sift out similar absurdities, it does not always manage it. The so-called Mandela Effect is an even greater blunder than a déjà vu and can't be put down to the memory glitch of a single individual.

This is when a very large group of people, literally millions, collectively misremembers something in the current reality, for which there is no factual confirmation. For example, many remember with all clarity that a certain phrase was spoken in such and such a film. And yet, now, that phrase has disappeared somewhere or been replaced and there is no record of it on any medium, even in the very earliest sources. There are numerous examples like this one, and not only in connection with films.

What can account for this? Mass confusion? Why does this happen? The answer is simply that our general reality has shifted to a different film roll in which there is a different version of that particular phrase. Reality accepts an unacceptable mistake: *the past has changed* without the address in the collective memory being corrected. The collective distinctly remembers what was on the previous film, because their addresses are still connected to it.

Here we should qualify this by saying that until now we have been talking about individual film rolls. Whereas in fact, the general film of reality is constructed in a much more complex manner. The individual film rolls of individual people turn separately, but they lie on a collective roll common to all humanity. The end of the world will affect us all, right? This has been predicted so many times and yet it still has not happened. As seers perceive it, this version of reality must exist somewhere in the archive, but for now, the collective human reality jumps onto another more fortuitous roll before the event can actually take place.

It can also be the case that the present enters the past. For example, the following is a well-documented fact. On 14th July,

1911 a passenger train departed from Rome on its way to Lombardy, and when on the way it entered a mountain tunnel, it disappeared without trace. At that time (more precisely, an even earlier time) the Mexican newspapers of 1840 paid witness to an unusual occurrence. One hundred and four Italians equipped with passports and attributes fitting to the period arrived in Mexico insisting that they had come from Rome by train. Of course, nobody believed them and they could think of nothing better than to hide them away on a psychiatric ward.

What happened to the reality of the missing Italians? Well, as we have already said, reality is something *that never was, never will be and only is, once and now.* And so it is. This case does not change anything because reality is always the current frame. But if this kind of anomaly occurs and different film rolls intersect somehow (and they can do completely at random), then a frame from the future may end up in a film roll from the past. Then, people and objects from that film roll appear in the past.

But how can this be?! The frame is moving consistently, one frame after the other! How can people who are born in the present die in the past which also moves in a specific sequence. Initially, the first frame ran in which the people disappeared. Then the second frame ran, in which they reappeared. Whereas in fact, the latter frame came first and the former frame ran second. It is just that the film rolls of the future and the past were mixed up causing the kind of aberration of perception that we are unaccustomed to and which remains incomprehensible despite all our attempts at an explanation.

However, there are also documented facts, concerning people from the past, who have turned up in the present with all their belongings right down to the contents of their pockets. There have also been cases in which archaeologists have found artefacts in their excavations that were produced recently or perhaps in an as yet unknown future. Here, again the film rolls have got mixed up and are intersecting. Sometimes, the film rolls do not so much intersect as just touch alongside each other. That is when you get a chronomirage.

Neither people nor objects time travel literally as material objects in space. They might not exist in reality at all, either the present or the past. But they can materialise anywhere and at any time if their film roll falls into the current frame of this place and time. *Material reality is the illuminated frame. Reality itself is a multitude of film rolls.* This is what needs to be understood.

These anomalies do not prove anything, but they do serve as indirect confirmation that reality is an infinite space made up of variations of different film rolls. Moreover, it follows that not only the quanta of the microcosm are discrete but all of reality, because the film rolls consist of frames separated at intervals from one another. If science would accept that the macrocosm as well as the microcosm was quantum, all sorts of new discoveries would be made. For example, instantaneous movement through time and space, as well as other anomalies occur in the spaces between frames.

All the practices we have covered confirm that all reality is discrete rather than continuous. Freeing yourself from the frame frequency of the current film roll, you acquire the ability to create the impossible. Literally, all these procedures with attention and the plait take you out of the frequency and phases of reality. And in this sense, you acquire the ability to stroll freely through a film.

One may suppose that the Eternity archive, did not appear instantly either but rather evolved over time. Everything that was or that could have been was not always recorded. (although one could also maintain, that the archive has always existed. Only then one has to delve into philosophy and determine the semantics of the word 'always'. What does 'always' mean? Does anyone know?)

Evolution is, in a certain sense, a process of producing information. Both living and non-living nature evolves, develops and simultaneously produces information about itself concerning the variants of its existence. The evolution of the Web is a good analogy — visitors type in their information and the data accumulates.

The film archive is not a comprehensive, totally infinite information field, which has always existed in relation to everything, but rather, let's say, *a part of infinity*, which moves and grows like a huge construct, which is also infinite. It moves and grows within infinity. *It's infinity as a part of infinity.* Can you imagine such a thing? No? And there's no need to. There is no point overanalysing things that are beyond the mind. (Who knows, someone may argue that infinity does not exist and the Universe is finite. But who can say for certain?)

Don't overthink things, instead, act and enjoy the feeling of delight simply from knowing that you are capable of recreating yourself and your own reality. This discovery of light at the end of the tunnel gives you strength, hope, and purpose, which also means, the energy for the intention to create such something that from the point of view of the average man in the street, 'is impossible'.

CONCLUSION

So, my good ones, we have come to the end of the first volume of our narrative. This is just the first volume and we will, of course, meet again.

If you have not yet transformed into fireflies, then, you are at least close to it and are currently somewhere in the transitionary phase of a lizard, an elusive, curious lizard!

You will bask in the rays of my glory, narrow your eyes, wag your tails, open your mouths wide, and make zoological sounds hissing: "Tufti-Tufti-i-i! Priestess-Priestess-ah,ah!" and then, gather in a flock and whisper to each other, whilst glancing back at me: "How can we use her in our own interests?!"

The most important thing is that you use the knowledge you have received. Most people (almost all) live without ever waking up. They go through life as if not of sound mind, without looking up or looking about them. They never try to create their own reality and just drift through the existing motion picture like a fish drifts around an aquarium.

Do you understand now how strikingly you differ? Don't forget though, that this does not give you the right to look down on others, or worse, behave towards them with contempt. Don't be sleeping characters. It is a worthless task. Let other people live as they want to and as they are able. Those who are capable of awakening will find me, just like you did. *Remember me and don't forget yourself.*

The knowledge described here is given in a very concentrated form and, what is more, it is the kind of knowledge that may appear too vague and elusive. You could let it wash over you without understanding it at all. The reason it is elusive is that it concerns an illusion, in which you are constantly immersed — the illusion of action which consists, if I may remind you, in that you think you live an independent life and are in complete control of your actions.

At the same time, nothing works out the way you want it to. Herein lie the contradiction and the paradox. If you act according to your will, why is it that everything turns out differently to how you would like it to? You think the reason things aren't working out is simply that they aren't working out, and that's it. In fact, the reason things aren't working out is that you are not in fact acting according to your will — you are being led by the script.

When you are taken over by anxiety, fear, dislike and other emotions, you are plunged into a dream, into a trance and are not yourself. You might think that it is these emotions that have taken control over you, but that is not the case. *Emotions immerse you in sleep and then the script owns you.*

The other reason that things are not working out is that you don't know how to act so that they do. Instead of composing your future reality, you fight with your current reality. The aim of this book is to drag you out of the illusion. There is not an

169

awful lot that needs to be said on the matter; it is better that you first understand, become aware and see wherein your illusion lies. This of itself will not be enough to radically change your life, but in the forthcoming books, you will be able to learn much more about it.

Every day there is something that bothers you, that makes you feel disheartened or oppressed. You have to catch yourself when these moments occur and redirect the vector of change *instead of giving in to them: 'I can create reality, and it is up to me to decide what the reality will look like'*. Remember that you are composing an end result, the goal frame, and not a specific course of events. Develop this habit.

Remember I said that power is a reality driver? This is what turns the film roll. If you start to compose reality, *power will notice you*. Power always focuses its attention on those who help turn the film roll. Power lifts them up and begins to help them. Power is not interested in empty dream mannequins, who play roles in films unawakened. Adopt the following motto: **'I look for power, I find power, and do everything with power'**. That is, I do everything powerfully, brilliantly and with soul. Do this, and then power will walk with you.

Be careful not to fall into a state of childish glee as you delight in your own miracles. Rejoice to yourself quietly, or reality might be tempted to take revenge (reality can be like that sometimes, a tad malicious), and even more importantly, avoid bragging about it to your friends.

Don't talk to your friends in conversation about the methods for creating your own reality and mannequins. They may not understand and then you will be laughed at. These techniques should not be looked at out of context. It is better to recommend that your friends read the book for themselves if they are curious about what you say. Do not lend your own copy as a book like this is a kind of talisman. This book is more than a collection of texts; it is a thing *that has power*. Hold it in your hands, feel its weight, and the overall sense of it. It is yours.

And I am Tufti! Farewell snails! Until we meet again in the following volumes!

METHODS

Why is it so important to carry out the methods described here? Because methods release you from the script, bring you to life in the film, and instil helpful automatic responses.

Awakening Method

1. You wake up, the moment something happens.
2. Before doing anything, you wake up.

Focus your attention on your awareness centre, on the point between the inner and outer screens. From here you can simultaneously observe your thoughts and what is happening around you. You can see your surrounding reality and yourself within that reality. Nothing prevents you from watching both screens at the same time. *You can do this.*

Examples of external triggers: you met with someone, someone asked you something, something happened close by; it doesn't matter what, any sound or movement — anything at all that would have attracted and involved you previously. As soon *as something* happens, focus your attention on it immediately, but do not lose control of your focus, hold it at the centre.

172

Examples of inner triggers: you are planning to go some-where, do something or talk to someone. Before you act, bring your attention to the awareness centre. It is important to do this beforehand because after you have taken action, it will be too late. You will simply discover that first you fell asleep, then woke up and realised that you were sleeping.

Frame Illumination Method

3. Catch yourself being affected by one of the triggers.
4. Wake up: I see myself and I see reality.
5. Activate the plait, without releasing the sensation of it, compose the reality you desire.
6. Drop the sensation of the plait.
7. If the event is significant, repeat the illumination several times.

In the same way that you tracked your attention, now keep track of the impending frame. Here there are three triggers:

Expectation — something is likely to happen, you are waiting, hoping for something.
Intention — you intend to go somewhere or do something.
Problem — something has happened that needs dealing with.

Whenever you are expecting something, don't wait or hope — compose your own reality. Whenever you intend do-ing something, do not hurry to start; first compose the reality you wish to see. Every time a problem arises, once again, don't wait, don't hope, don't fuss, compose the reality you wish to experience.

The frame illumination method is an exercise in develop-ing meta-power and, at the same time, a means of composing the reality you want. Follow the illumination method calmly and naturally. Use thoughts, words, visualisation — whatever works best for you. The most effective type of illumination is visualisation.

Plait With Flow Method

1. Take an in-breath, and on the out-breath, imagine the arrow moving at an angle away from your back. Now the plait is activated.
2. Without letting go of the sensation of the plait, compose a picture of your reality. At the same time, make sure that you are breathing freely.
3. Without losing the sense of the plait (the arrow), take an in-breath and on the out-breath sharply send the arrow into a vertical downward position, triggering both energy flows.
4. Staying aware of the movement of the rising and descending energy flows, say the following thought form quietly to yourself or aloud: My intention is being realised.
5. Then let go of all the sensations you have been working with.

What is happening when you do this? You are not only composing your own reality with the help of the plait, you are putting out (sending) your intention as a 'message' to the universe. In this way, the energy flow strengthens the work of the plait. If this technique works for you and you enjoy it, you can use this variation of the exercise all the time. But if not, then the basic method will be sufficient.

Advantage Method

1. Catch yourself at the non-acceptance trigger.
2. Wake up: I see myself and I see reality.
3. Ask yourself: what is the advantage in this?
4. If an answer comes to you, accept it and take the advantage.

5. If no answer comes to you, try to accept the idea of advantage anyway.

Every event or situation, whatever its nature, has a positive side and a negative side.

The script is not trying to cause you harm at all because inflicting harm takes energy. The script always takes the path of least resistance. But you give a knee-jerk, non-accepting reaction either due to your nasty character, your propensity for negativity, your habit of self-protection, your high opinion of yourself, or even just because 'nothing is going your way'! As a result, as usual, you spoil your own life and the life of those around you.

More than this, the script works to achieve your goal if you set a goal. When you compose your own reality, the script aligns itself according to your composition even if it does not appear to you that this is the case. But you always insist that everything should go exactly according to your plan, and thereby obstruct the implementation of the plan.

Adopt and integrate one simple principle: *seek out the advantage in everything*. Literally, seek and draw out the advantage in any annoying situation, and in any event that causes you to respond even a little bit negatively. Set yourself this goal: draw out the advantage.

But in order for this to work, you need to wake up and shift your attention to the centre. The triggers in this case are mostly external: someone says something to you, does something, or around you something is going on — anything that causes your non-acceptance, from slight dissatisfaction to absolute fury. Trigger emotions may also include irritation, depression, anxiety, aggression, and fear.

To make the right choice, you only need to stop and think for a moment: *what might the advantage be in this?* And then, do not resist the script, try and follow it. Literally, follow advice given to you, heed opinions expressed, agree, go to something, and accept things you would have previously rejected or caused you to enter into a possible confrontation.

As a result, you are transported to an alternative film roll, where, in contrast, everything works to your advantage, because you stopped at the right moment and chose to benefit from the advantage of the situation. It is all very simple: what you choose is what you receive.

In reality there is one immutable law. The law is this: *the more you allow yourself to be guided by the principle of advantage, the fewer events life will throw at you that are harmful.*

The Following Method

1. Catch the moment of the control trigger.
2. Wake up: I see myself and I see reality.
3. Ask yourself, sense, what is the first dictate telling you?
4. If an answer comes to you, follow the dictate.
5. If no answer comes to you, compose the goal frame and try following again.

Being endowed with self-awareness, you are constantly asking the question 'how?' and then you conjure up a whole strategy for achieving what you desire. Yes, in the moments that you ask yourself this question, your self-awareness awakens, but it hinders you because in your mind, rather than holding sight of the goal, you focus on your own silly ideas of how to achieve it. You spoil everything by insisting on having things your own way.

What you must keep in mind is not a specific course of events or people's behaviour (actions) but the end result — the goal frame. You should observe yourself, and where you place your attention, to prevent it from fabricating its own plan and, instead, follow the subtle nudges of the script taking them to be the dictates of Power.

By consciously allowing the script to lead you, you are in fact leading yourself, using the Power and Wisdom of the script. And then everything goes smoothly and well. It's when you don't allow it to lead you that you end up spoiling everything. It turns out that 'nothing is going my way' in part because you are not allowing it to.

Here you can use all the triggers which we included in the attention tracking method, frame illumination and advantage methods. You should make regular use of all the triggers until it becomes habit. This is the only way to learn to wake up at the right moment. If you don't adopt this habit, nothing will happen. The ability to wake up at the right moment is essential.

In addition to the above, I'll mention the control triggers. Your most harmful habit is your desire to control everything: the script, events, other people.

1. I want something from people and events.
2. I want everything to go according to my plan.
3. Something is not turning out the way I wanted it to.

The habit of 'controlling' must be replaced with a new habit of letting go and following.

The Image Method

As soon as you find yourself wanting something from someone, wake up and stand in front of the mirror. What do you need to do for the reflection to meet you half way? Take the first step. *Give to others, what you would like to receive.*

1. Catch yourself thinking: I want other people to give me something.
2. Be fully present: wanting is futile, you have to give.
3. Ask yourself: what can I give that is the same?
4. If you find something similar, give it now and give upfront.
5. If you don't find something similar, then just give anyway.

Use the following table to compose the image you want:

You want:	*Compose the image by:*	*Reflection gives:*
Fun time with friends.	*Listening carefully.*	*People socialise with you.*
Be interesting.	*Showing interest*	*People are interested in you.*
Receive help and support.	*Helping others.*	*People help you.*
People understand you.	*Trying to understand others.*	*People understand you.*
People are compassionate towards you.	*Showing compassion.*	*People reciprocate*
Gaining approval.	*Showing approval.*	*People approve of you.*
Gaining respect.	*Giving respect.*	*You are respected.*
Receiving gratitude.	*Showing gratitude.*	*You are appreciated.*
Being liked by others.	*Being kind.*	*People like you.*
Being admired by others.	*Showing admiration.*	*People admire you.*
Being loved.	*Being loving.*	*You are loved.*

178

Simply line up all your thoughts and actions with a plus sign after them. All your 'give me's' have a minus sign after them and either don't work or create the opposite effect. Similarly, all your negative thoughts and actions come back to you like a boomerang.

What you don't want:	*Don'ts:*
Encountering aggressive types	*Don't show aggression*
Being criticised	*Don't criticise others*
Feeling judged	*Don't judge others*
Suffering damage	*Don't harm others*
Being afraid	*Don't make threats*
Having an unpleasant personality	*Don't cause trouble*

There is a general principle for composing the image: *rather than complaining to the world, love it.* In reality, all you need is love. It's just that you don't always understand these words in the right context. You want people to love you. You think that first people will love you and then you will love the world. But it should be the other way round: you love, you radiate love, without demanding anything in return, and only then can love come to you.

The Reflection Method

In a three-dimensional mirror, the subject and the reflection are connected. So what does that give us? It means that the image you create can become a reflection, and the reflection can flow into the subject. In other words, *you can turn a reflection into a subject pretending you have something you don't, or that you are someone, you have not yet become.*

For example, you want to have your own home. You wander round the shops looking at furniture and items to decorate the interior as if you already had a home. Or you might want to be wealthy. You look at expensive things, cars, yachts, spa resorts. Allow wealth into your life. Or you want to become a star in some area or another. Behave as if you were already a star; live that life, for now at least, in your imagination.

Don't worry that it might feel like a game or self-deception. If you are serious in your approach to the game, reality will be forced to take you seriously. It is a mirror after all! *Your task is to be present and feel now how you would feel if you already had what you want, or already were the person you'd like to be.* Fake it and live out the faking of it. It's make-believe, but it's no joke. No joke, you see?

Gradually, the picture of reality will attune itself to your make-believe. Reality loves to create illusions, but it can't stand being fed them. It will find a way of turning the illusion you have created into reality.

1. Catch yourself thinking: I want something or to be someone.
2. Become fully present: wanting is futile, you have to start composing.
3. Fake it and behave as if you had already achieved what you desire.

What you imitate is what you get; who you pretend to be is who you will become. Live it in your thoughts, in virtual space, and where possible, in your actions, in reality, until you totally believe in the illusion you have created. As soon as you believe in it, reality will believe in it too.

There are just two necessary conditions: *the first is to take the game seriously; the second is to play the game consistently.*

Design Synchronisation Method

You are created according to your DNA pattern and the design, which, being located in the information space, you can adjust. The design can change for the better or the worse, depending on your condition. Condition refers to your sense of self, who you really are, warts and all. Your condition is more than a passing mood, it's your sense of self.

So, regardless of the initial parameters of the design, you can turn from a darling of fate into a very unattractive brat, or, the opposite, transform from an ugly duckling into everyone's favourite. If you drift, weak-willed, along with the script, like the incompetent characters of a film, you will fly, if you are fortunate and you will fall, if something goes wrong.

The fact is, that you either control your condition, *or it is controlled for you.* You should intentionally choose your condition. You shift into a new condition by carrying out the three types of movement (propel reality, propel yourself, propel yourself from within).

But for now, this new condition is nothing more than imitation. You will shift into a genuine (rather than an imitated) condition when you start to see confirmation that the technique really works. This is why I so strongly recommend that you always pay special attention to any shifts you notice taking place. As soon as you spot a change, immediately activate the plait and savour your achievements, taking pleasure in all the details. *In this moment, your condition synchronises with design and the design is adjusted.* **This means, that you are occupying a new mannequin.**

In a genuine condition, your thought forms are transformed into thought markers:

Every day, I get closer to achieving my goal.

181

Really, I do everything brilliantly. My professionalism is growing.
I really am getting physically fitter.
I really am become a more charming and attractive person.

Thought markers are confirmation of the fact that shifts can take place.

1. Carry out all three actions, separately or simultaneously.
2. Observe carefully and avidly grasp any confirmation of your success.
3. As soon as you see a sign of success, activate the plait and consolidate the shift with a thought marker.

Thought forms trigger a new reality; thought markers adjust the design.

Integrated Action-stroll Method

1. Composing a new reality and yourself within it.
2. Pretend that you already live in that reality and that you are already that new self.
3. And, of course, act, create that new self, fan the Creator's Spark.

This is what we talked about earlier; it is what you are capable of doing inside the film: propel the forthcoming frame, propel yourself, propel yourself from within. Take it all seriously, practice consistently and for a relatively long period of time — always. Then, one film roll at a time, one reflection at a time, your mannequin and your life will begin to change. You will see change, of that there is no doubt.

REVIEW OF BASIC PRINCIPLES

The dream space is not a product of your imagination. It is real and exists in the form of a film archive, *where everything that was, is and ever might be is stored*. When you are seeing a dream, you are viewing one of these film rolls.

Physical reality is *not that which never was, nor that which never will be*, but rather that which happens, once and now. Physical reality exists for a single moment, like a frame in a film roll, which moves from the past into the future.

Reality is multi-layered, like an onion. Only two layers are familiar to you: physical reality, in which you live, and the dream space, which you dream about every night. Sleeping and waking are roughly the same thing, only they take place in different dimensions. Drifting off and waking up, you shift from one dimension into the other. Sleep and the awakening that follows sleep are similar in context to things like life and death. Life is sleeping, death is awakening and not the other way around.

Your life, more precisely, your essence — your soul — also moves from one incarnation to another. You do not remember your previous incarnations. This is because every incarnation a separate life of your soul, or a separate dream if you like. The presence of the body is not essential to the life of the soul. The soul in the body is just one of the forms in which the soul can exist. The body is a kind of bio-suit.

Movement and transformation are the fundamental qualities or reality and life. The frame moves along the film roll. The caterpillar transforms into a butterfly. The butterfly lays its larvae, which in turn are transformed into caterpillars to become butterflies again.

Inner screen When you are lost in thought, your attention is wholly immersed in the inner screen. You may be oblivious to what is going on around you and do things on auto-pilot.

Outer screen When your attention is busy with something external, you forget yourself and you do things automatically without having to think about it.

Attention Your attention is always focused either within or outside of yourself but very rarely in between. And so you are constantly sleeping. Your attention is used to being glued to one screen or the other, without pausing in the middle. The result of this is that you have stopped taking any control of your attention; it does not obey you, but drifts randomly about, you are constantly dropping into a non-conscious state.

Sleep Sleep is a subconscious state in which your attention is immersed either in the outer or the inner screen. In this state, you are helpless and have no control over yourself or indeed anything that is happening around you. *Sleep is your anabiotic state.*

Dreaming is what you see either in the dream space or in the space of physical reality. Reality and dreaming are essentially the same thing. For you are also dreaming reality. Reality is a dream, and dreaming is reality.

Awakening In order to wake up either in a dream or in waking life, you must pull your attention away from the external or internal screen and shift it to your awareness centre. See the 'Awakening method'.

The awareness centre is an observation point from which you can see where your attention is directed in any given moment and what it is focusing on. At the same time, you see what you are doing and what is going on around you.

Awareness Wake up and ask yourself: where am I, what am I doing, what is my attention immersed in? In the moment you ask yourself the question, you awaken and arrive at the awareness point. This is me, and this is my reality. I am aware. I see myself and I see my reality.

A stroll through a dream (asleep or in waking life) Enter the awareness point, having said to yourself: *I see myself and I see reality*. Tell yourself: today I will take a stroll through a waking dream. And then go for a stroll anywhere, to work or to school, in this state of clarity. When you are immersed in either one of the screens, you aren't there; you aren't in control of yourself or the situation. In a condition of clarity, you are free, and from this moment your dream, whether it be whilst sleeping or in waking life, becomes lucid. You are in control of yourself, and most importantly, acquire the capacity to control the situation.

Film characters — that's you. As asleep, as in waking life, you are in a film and you are carried by the flow of the script. *Your mind is not your own, because your attention is not your own.* On your stroll, you ought to have noticed that your own attention was constantly drifting away either to the outer or the inner screen. When you are aware, unlike the other characters around you who are asleep, you see yourself, you see reality, and can consciously control your will, which you couldn't previously. This is your first step towards a new level of self-control and control of your own reality.

Script You are led by a certain outer script, which weaves you into a film, in which you are one of the characters.

Dream characters How are dream characters different to living people (film characters)? They have no self-awareness — they are not aware of themselves as individual personalities. They have no willpower — they are not free in their actions; they are controlled by the script. They have no soul. They are simply templates, mannequins. They cannot say 'I am me'. They have no self.

You, or rather, your Self, is the same thing as your attention. Your attention cannot stay in the awareness centre for very long. You have to develop the new habit of bringing your attention back to the centre. Use your attention to track your attention, yourself that is.

Dreams (both whilst sleeping and in waking life) can be either *lucid or non-lucid*. In a non-lucid dream, you are dotty and helpless, like a rabbit. But all you have to do is start controlling the focus of your attention and you come to life in a movie, gaining the ability to behave at will, exactly as you see fit.

Triggers You do not have to try and hold your attention in the awareness centre continuously. Meaning and value are to be found in something else, namely your ability to respond to what is going on around you. You need to acquire the opposite habit — not to fall into a dream but *to wake up when something happens around you*. Any event, even a slight waft of air in your space, should make you alert — this is an awakening signal.

Likewise, any action you take should be a reminder to check where your attention is focused. Example triggers:

Outer — as soon as something happens, you wake up.
Inner — before you do anything, wake up.

Eternity archive Same thing goes for the dreaming space, which exists in the form of a film roll archive, where everything is stored *that ever was, will be and could be.* Only the illuminated frame, a momentary impression of physical reality, is truly real. Everything else is virtual, including the past and the future. And all this is stored in the Eternity archive.

Compose reality *To compose reality means to determine the direction in which the frame will move and the film roll that will be played. You have the opportunity to do this,* but you don't make the most of it, just as you don't use your attention control function. You have to compose your desired reality in advance, rather than battling with your current circumstances. Instead, you try and change the given reality of the current frame. Reality is only 'reality' by virtue of the fact that it has already happened. *You cannot change anything that has already happened.* But this is exactly what you try to do, in as much as everything *that surrounds you consists of that which has already happened.*

Propel the frame As you know, changing the past is impossible. You may as well forget about the present too as that also has already happened and it isn't what you would choose. What you do have is the chance to create your own future and choose a film roll, along which the next frame will move.

Intention Intention accounts for your actions. In order to start anything, you have to first intend it. When you are doing something, intention is implemented via action. Similarly to attention, which has two screens, intention has two centres, an inner and an outer centre.

*The inner centre accounts for all your everyday function-
ing and is located in the frontal part of the skull — this is your
petty intention.* When you concentrate, you frown. When you
intend to do something, you tense your muscles. Your muscles
enable you to take basic forms of action in the current frame.

You hardly use the outer centre at all. Yet this is what moves
the future frame. You can see where the outer centre is located
in an instant, right now.

The intention plait This is an energy chakra, and similarly
to a normal plait — you cannot see it, but you can feel it like
you would a phantom limb, which is no longer there, but you
still feel as if it was. Rather than hanging down, it sticks out at
an angle from the spine.

The outer intention centre is at the end of the plait. This place
it between the shoulders, only not right against the spine but a
little away from it. You should be able to find the spot intuitively.
The exact distance away from the spine is not important. Just
focus your attention on this area and you will feel it.

*The principle of the outer intention centre works is really
very simple.* You shift your attention to the end of the plait and
visualise a picture of any event that you would like to attract
into your life. Doing this you illuminate this future frame, and
it becomes manifest in physical reality.

See chapter 'Plait with flow'.

How to work with the plait *First: wake up and shift to the
awareness point.* As usual, say to yourself: I see myself and I
see reality.

Second: activate the plait. Feel it. There it is; as soon as you
focus your attention on it, the plait lifts away from the spine
and is activated.

*Third: still focusing your attention on the plait, imagine a
picture of the future you want.* Compose the picture of your
reality in thoughts, words, and on the screen — as best as
you can.

188

This is how you illuminate the future frame and it manifests into physical reality.

The illusion of action It only appears to you, that you are in control of your actions. It is a very plausible thought but still an illusion. *What is illusory is not only what you think you see, but also, what you think you do.* You cannot tell that this is an illusion because you are constantly immersed in it.

What do you think, do the fictional characters of films and computer games understand that they are in a film and that you are watching them? No. Are the mannequins in your dreams aware, that you are dreaming them? No. And so now I ask you: *do you know who you are?*

You cannot ask film characters this question. You can ask a mannequin, but there's no point. You differ from the former and the latter in that you are at least capable of vaguely grasping the meaning of the question. And in that, you are capable of having self-awareness. But **when** are you self-aware? Only in the moment that you ask yourself this question. The rest of the time, where are you and who are you?

Well, you are characters in a filmstrip of the life that is happening to you. *Rather than living your life, life is happening to you.* Neither the mannequin in your dream, nor the hero in a film are capable of perceiving the illusion of their actions, or rather, the illusion of action. So why should you assume that you are capable of doing so? How are you different to a dream mannequin if you live as if you were sleeping in waking life?

Habit You are made snails (more precisely, characters) through the habit *of not creating your own reality but waiting and hoping for something instead.* Will it happen or not? Will it work out or not? This is a passive position. From this position, all you are capable of is probing reality and at the slightest thing, withdrawing your horns.

The mould You have to switch into proactive mode. *Rather than waiting and hoping, create the reality you want.*

189

The **mould** is an obstacle to this, because according to the mould, creating your own reality is impossible. The mould is your little house. New habits and perceptions are developed just as the old ones took root — through ongoing repetition. Only from now on, instead of staring at reality and following it, you will actively manage the movement of the frame — not the one in which you currently find yourself, but the one that is about to come up. See. 'Frame illumination method'.

Reprogramming *It is your snail horns and house (habit and the mould)* that keep you trapped in the current frame. In order to escape the trap, you must switch to proactive mode, not waiting and hoping, and compose the reality you want. This requires constant practice of how to manage the impending frame. Method: as soon as you find yourself waiting or expecting something, use intention; as soon as a problem arises, use instant plait activation and frame illumination. You need to compose not only the events, of which the outcome is unknown, but also events of which the outcome is already probable.

Why do we need endless repetition? To embed a new programme into your snail mould. You will not believe that reality can submit to your will, until you experience it for yourself, moreover, repeatedly. Controlling frame movement in simple events is the most effective type of training, as a result of which you will...

– Learn to wake up and control your attention.
– Develop the plait, visualisation and intention.
– Switch to proactive mode, and in the end, acquire the ability to free yourself from the predominant script and compose your own reality.

Forthcoming reality although written in the Eternity archive, is always multi-variant and while it has not been ultimately claimed or composed by anyone, it does not belong to any one. If someone comes along and composes it, then it will submit to their composition. And if that someone is you, then it will be yours. But before reality can truly become yours, you have to reprogram yourself, i.e., develop new habits and perceptions via a process of multiple repetition.

Transformation *The Creator conceived you to be luminescent creatures, your gaze* directed forward. And so you once were, before you became mired in the illusion of action. When you practice composing your own reality, you become gradually transformed from snails into fireflies. When you illuminate the frame, you emit an inner light, and the events you desire fly towards you, like moths to a flame. Others around you, who are still snails, will put their horns out towards you and crawl closer out of curiosity.

Concentration Try without making an effort. To illuminate a frame successfully, *concentration is important,* not force. Can you concentrate, at least for a couple of minutes? Just a minute, then? That is all it requires of you. Follow the illumination method calmly and naturally. The reason for this is that by applying effort, you trigger the inner intention centre. Reality is managed from the outer centre.

Note that if whilst you are illuminating the frame, your muscles are tense, this means your petty intention is working. You have to work exclusively with outer intention — with the plait. This is not something that should be strained or wielded.

Meta-power This is the flip side of force, its antipode. Normal force (willpower and physical strength) works from this side of the mirror reality, the material plane, while meta-power operates from the other side, the subtle plane.

The reflection in the mirror reality is on this side, the material plane, while the subject is on the other side, the subtle plane.

Physical reality is a reflection of the subject, the image, which is somewhere there, on the other side. And there, in the film archive, there are many variants of the future.

So, now, judge for yourself: if the future is located on the other side of the reality mirror, is it possible to somehow have an impact on it using standard force, which only operates here on the side the mirror is facing? No.

If your attention is focused on what is in front of the mirror, i.e. in the frame of manifestation, then you are completely captured by the script. If it is focused on the other side of the mirror, in the image frame, then you are free to move, both yourself, and future reality.

You will gradually come to understand what meta-power is, as you come to feel it. I would not be able to explain to you what power was if you had never tasted it. The same goes for meta-power. You have to feel it and develop it. The plait is your meta-power tool. The frame illumination method is an exercise in developing meta-power and, at the same time, a means of composing the reality you want.

Propel yourself To propel yourself means to be self-aware and deliberately control your motives and your actions. Within the frame, you will move normally, using your arms, legs, and physical strength. But you propel reality completely differently, with your attention, *intention, and meta-power.*

Imitating action The point of imitation lies in the fact that you do not have the right to disrupt the established order of things. The established order has it that you participate in the action *whilst submitting to the lines of the script.* There is not a single character that can bail out of the film roll or do whatever they like within the film. The script is not the product of someone's subjective will. It is an objective reality and there's no avoiding the fact.

Objective reality is such that you are doomed to exist within it, like characters in a film. You cannot avoid the action. But you can imitate it. You can fool reality.

You continue to play your role as before, as it is written into the script; you carry out your daily tasks. But unlike the other characters, being in a state of awareness, you get something more — the opportunity to replace the current film roll.

192

You stroll through the film as a character that has come to life but is pretending to be lifeless, and change the film roll as you see fit. No-one suspects anything — neither the script, nor the other characters.

Presence in the film Your presence in the film is above all, the presence of your awareness, your 'Self'. Your presence as a living, self-aware, conscious individual in full possession of your faculties in an immutable film. Although the film turns dynamically, it is predetermined, like the behaviour of all its characters.

Your presence in the film singles you out as one awakened among those who are asleep. You are conscious of your separateness and are aware of what is happening. Your behaviour within the film is also predetermined by the script. However, your presence gives you the opportunity to change the film roll — to skip from one to another.

In order to become present, you must come alive, give yourself a good shake and work out where your attention is placed: in the central awareness point or one of the two screens.

You are not in control of the script Composing reality is not about controlling the script but choosing the film roll. Your task is to hold your attention on the frame that is coming next. The script is none of your business. If you try to compose it or resist it, the script will pull you into its trap. Trying to influence the course of events, you make the mistake of taking the reality of the current frame in a deadly grip. The harder you grip, the tighter it grabs you by the tail, that is, by the plait.

It is not for you to know, what script will bring you to your goal. But the point is that you don't need to know. You are working in a film projector mode. *When the goal frame is illuminated by your projector, the course of events itself turns to where you need it to be. The script works for your goal if you set it.*

Advantage You always insist on everything going according to your plan, and in so doing, you obstruct the implementation of the plan. By expressing dislike, you involuntarily and unconsciously compose a worse reality for yourself.

To avoid mangling your reality, and instead, turning it into a wonderful world in all regards, you need to implement one simple principle: *seek the advantage in everything*. Literally, seek and draw out the advantage in any annoying situation, and in any event that causes you to respond even a little bit negatively. Set yourself the goal of seeking out the advantage in life.

The Law has it: *if you allow yourself to be guided by the principle of advantage, life will throw fewer and fewer events your way that are damaging*. See 'Advantage method'.

Allowing The paradoxical principle: *compose not the script but the goal frame. Your job is to know the 'result' you want to achieve and compose the corresponding picture of that reality, in thoughts, words, and images using the plait. Then the script will lead you and show you the 'how'*.

Tracking the advantage is one trigger for awakening. Any event you experience should be something that causes you to be alert serving as a wake-up call, rather than sending you off to sleep. Your task *is to wake up, see reality and compose reality*.

Previously, as soon as anything challenging happened, you'd 'A-a-a!', wave your arms about, and stamp your feet!

Now: as soon as something challenging happens, you exclaim (quietly to yourself, or aloud) 'Advantage!'

Beyond that, you allow the universe to do something nice for you, to help you, or to bring you a step closer to your goal.

The script directs you Why are you constantly forgetting about your attention? Is it down to absent-mindedness? No. It is because you are being directed by the script. You think you are acting independently and that you know what's what, but this is an illusion. The illusion of action, let me remind you, consists in the fact, that reality takes hold of you to the extent that you do not notice the illusion and don't realise that you are bound characters in some kind of game.

The paradox is that unlike the heroes in the film, you are endowed with the quality of self-awareness. *However, you become self-aware, only in the moment that you ask yourself this question*. The rest of the time, your consciousness sleeps and relinquishes itself to the external script.

Propel yourself Imagine that you are a character in a film. The film roll is turning and you cannot change the plot, but nothing is to stop you from changing yourself. Do not listen to people who tell you that you must never change. To a certain degree, they are right, you must never lose a sense of your core, your originality, your uniqueness.

You have to change, without changing your Self. Working on self-improvement doesn't mean compromising your true self. Nature originally created you perfect, warts and all, like everyone else. But lack *of development leads to degradation.* It is a natural law. You should be aware, that you need to work on yourself, develop yourself physically and spiritually unless you want to turn into shrivelled slugs.

The Creator's Spark Much depends on your self-improvement. In each and every one of you there lies a tiny part of the Creator — the Creator's Spark — so kindle it! It is the Spark, not of the Lord but of the Creator. To lord it over others is another kind of temptation. Which you must never give in to. Create your reality and yourself perfect. The Supreme Creator does not contradict this rule; he does not rule over you (what would be the point, you wouldn't listen anyway), he creates, and you are capable of doing the same.

The dictates of Power Having the capacity for self-awareness, you ask the question 'how?' and design a whole strategy for achieving your goal based on your own ideas. Yes, in the moment that you ask yourself 'how,' your self-awareness is awakened, but it gets in your way because you're not thinking about the goal but your own silly ideas of how to manifest it. Your imagined script contradicts the real one, but you insist on having your own way and spoil everything as a result. The scenario you have invented conflicts with the real one, but you spoil everything by insisting on having things your own way.

You need to observe yourself, observe your attention so that rather than sinking back into thoughts of your own plan, you follow the barely perceptible nudges from the script as if they were dictates of Power. You can sense these dictates of Power if you allow them to lead you, consciously and intentionally. If your thoughts are focused solely on the goal, the script will lead you to the goal itself.

Following *Your mind should be focused on the end result, the goal frame, not the course of events or the behaviour* (actions) of other people. You can't resist the script even when you are fully present. All the changes that take place in your reality that occur according to your will, are the result of you switching to a different film roll. You can't do anything about the script in the current film roll. Don't resist the script, observe yourself and follow the flow of the film roll. Learn to feel the dictates of Power and to follow the dictates of Power. *Follow* in order to make the most of the Power and Wisdom of the script. See 'The following method'.

Outer Power *You are strolling live through a film when you are present with your attention, and move with intention.* Move the frame, but not with your petty intention, move it with outer intention. Outer intention is referred to as such because it is not yours; it does not belong to you or submit to your will. Outer intention is a kind of Power, *the engine that is powering reality.* Its active component turns the film roll in the way it is destined to turn.

You have an access point to this power which is your outer centre, the plait. When you are asleep, Power takes you by the plait and leads you through the script as if you were a puppet. But when you are awake, fully present and take the plait 'into your own hands', meta-power, Power's reactive component, is

196

activated. This is what enables you to launch a different film roll, one that corresponds to the frame you are composing.

The reality mirror You always go at things head on, acting from a place of petty intention. When you want people to love, respect, and help you, to give you something, you tend to demand it directly like a child: 'love me', 'respect me', 'help me', 'give me'.

From the outside, this is what the scene looks like: you are standing in front of a mirror, reaching out your hands and shouting "Give it to me!", trying to pull the reflection closer. The reflection responds by doing the same. It does not give, it takes away. In reality, as in the mirror, you always get the reflection of all your mental attitudes and actions. *As the message, so the response.* Particularly, when you are expressing a negative response with all your heart. As a rule, reality gives a mirrorlike response. *What you give out, is what you get back.*

Composing the image *The first thing* you must do, in order to shoot your own film is to wake up, *and become fully present.* Imagine that you have come to life in a motion picture. Instead of watching the film, you are living in it. Feel it. Open your eyes and look around you as if for the first time. Look at everything afresh. You will notice that the colours are richer. Now, imagine yourself to be an objective outsider rather than a film character. You entered the film as an insider. Nobody else knows but you. Your body is inside the film, but your attention is outside it. *Feel your separateness, your presence.*

Second. Before you start wanting, expecting, and asking something of other people and reality, you must imagine that you are standing in front of a mirror and asking yourself the question: *what must I do for the reflection to meet me half way?* Obviously, you must take the first step. Instead of your usual manner of claiming the larger portion of the cake for yourself and harping on "give, give, give...", you wake up and realise that the reality mirror is simply repeating your movements. And if you want to receive something, you must first give something similar.

197

It doesn't matter what exactly. Simply, replace your 'give me' with the opposite, 'here, take'. And then, as if by magic, in the reflection, you will receive the very thing you wanted. *What you give out is what you get back.* This also **propelling yourself from within**. See 'The image method'.

You can control reality, but you can't control people If, when composing the goal frame, you try and forcibly make a certain individual dance to your tune, it probably won't work or it will produce the opposite effect, because you're breaking the rules twofold — you're intruding into someone else's script.

Only your personal reality is yours to play with. Therefore, only you should be the central figure in the goal frame as you imagine yourself in your dreams: you are the star on the stage, you are in the Director's chair, you are sailing your own yacht. All the other figures in the frame should be in the background, as part of the set design.

Trying to carry out these techniques involving specific people is not right. All you can do is have a mirror-like relationship with them. If you want something specific from a certain person, go and see them and communicate with them within the current film, taking account of the fact that the film is mirror-like in nature.

Inner motivator You are led not only by an outer driver, i.e. the script, but also by a certain inner motivator which is the need for a sense of self-worth and the pursuit of self-realisation. *If you want people to be well-disposed towards you, or you want something from them, set yourself the goal of underlining their importance and help them realise their own goals.*

If you want to avoid making enemies, *be very careful not to injure anyone else's sense of worth. Creating advantage for others should become part of your philosophy of life*. If you do this, you will have no difficulty with your own self-realisation. Moreover, your own realisation will be successful only *when it starts to benefi t others*. Conversely, if what you do is of no benefit to others, it won't really help you much either.

Manipulating others It is possible to manipulate the consciousness of another character in the current frame. As you are already aware, you are led both by the external script and an inner driving force. The latter, however, to a far lesser degree. This driving force mainly determines the direction in which you move, but you are still set in motion by the script. However, the most greedy snails, either in accordance with their intentions or their script may try to alter the direction your course is taking to suit their own interests.

This is manipulation — trying to control someone else's course in the film. This may be, for example, by deception, creating false values and goals, or by playing on the weaknesses and needs of others. Unlike the mirror principles that do not disturb your course, but rather assist it, manipulators will divert you from your course and use you. Whenever you feel that something is being imposed on you, ask yourself: *who does this benefit and how*?

Manipulating reality Reality has a dual nature. On the one hand, it is a film, and on the other hand, a three-dimensional mirror. Both are bound to confuse. *The main illusion is that the true nature of reality is hidden.* You can't see the space of a film strip, and the mirror framework itself isn't visible. But if you know this and you remember it, then the illusion will no longer have any power over you.

The illusion of the reality mirror is much more complex than a standard mirror. The space is not split in half, and there is no visible boundary between what is real and what is imaginary. *You are, at the same time, both inside and outside of the mirror.* The image and the mirror reflection are connected. So what does that give us? It means that the image you create can become a reflection, and the reflection can flow into the subject. In other words, *you can turn a reflection into a subject pretending you have something you don't, or that you are someone, you have not yet become.*

For example, you want to have your own home. You wander round the shops looking at furniture and items to decorate the interior as if you already had a home. Or you might want to be wealthy. You look at expensive things, cars, yachts, spa resorts. Allow wealth into your life. Or you want to become a star in some area or another. Behave as if you were already a star; live that life, for now at least, in your imagination.

Gradually, the picture of reality will attune itself to your make-believe. Reality loves to create illusions, but can't stand being fed them. It will find a way of turning the illusion you have created into reality.

Composing a reflection You are capable of composing both an image and a reflection. In the first case, the image appears as a reflection, whereas in the second, the opposite is true, the reflection appears as the image.

First (direct) process: what you put out is what you get back; what you give is what you receive, and who you really are is what you have.

Second (reverse) process: as the game, so the reality; what you imitate is what you get; who you pretend to be is who you will become.

Directly: the image appears as the reflection. Composing the image is your way of putting a message out to reality. What you put out is what you have.

Reversed: the reflection appears as the image. Your make-believe and imitation is your way of composing the reflection. Who you have pretended to be is, in reality, the person you have become.

All these manipulations with the mirror are what is being referred to when we talk about 'propelling yourself from within'.

The first essential condition is that the game is taken very seriously.

The second essential condition is that the game should be consistent.

See chapter 'The Reflection Method'.

The reason you do not like yourself The reason you don't like yourself is that all the screens and printed covers illustrate the ideals of beauty, success, and happiness. You fall for these illusions obediently trying to fit yourself into someone else's image, each time coming to the conclusion that you fall short of these standards. In actual fact, beauty, success, and happiness cannot be standardised; these things have a very individual cut. Yet, still, you prefer to believe in the illusion and try to keep up with it.

Don't be jealous when you look at others; and don't be discouraged when you look at yourself; become like fireflies: *propel yourself and propel yourself from within*. Don't look at the reality in which you find yourself living as something that is beyond your control; instead, compose a new one yourself. Shift your forthcoming reality by using the plait, and shift your current reality by moving yourself with the image you visualise and the reflection.

This is what is getting you down As soon as you have caught yourself waiting for something, hoping for something, being anxious about something, or burdened by something, wake up and be self-aware: you are being led by the external script, not your own script; this is what is getting you down. You feel subconsciously that you are not free, that you are dependent on reality, that you are limited by circumstances like a character is limited by a plot. You may sense it, but you cannot do anything about it because you are not fully aware.

You have to get to the point where you truly know that holding out for something to happen or not happen, to work out or not work out, is foolish and pointless. It is within the power of your will to compose a subject image, or a reflection, or reality, or all of these things at the same time. You should:

Replace the habit of wanting with the habit of giving.
Replace the habit of rejecting with the habit of accepting.
Replace the habit of dropping off with the habit of waking up.

The most beneficial habit is this: *don't want things of reality; compose reality*. That's the main thing but with equally important derivatives:

201

Don't be afraid, compose instead.
Don't wait, compose instead.
Don't hope, compose instead.
Don't lament, compose instead.

Imitation technique *It is possible to compose not only reality but yourself, your mannequin. And at the same time, the mannequin will change. By shifting in turn the film roll and the reflection, you will become different, the way you dreamed of seeing yourself.* See 'The integrated movement-strolling method', and chapter 'The Imitation Technique'.

Compose your own mannequin You have your own mannequins in the films, which are stored in the Eternity archive. When you see one of these film rolls in a dream, your consciousness finds your own mannequin, and then it comes to life and starts to move. For as long as you dream the dream, you occupy the body of the dream mannequin, as one of many of your potential variants.

The same thing happens in physical reality, in the film rolls, according to which your life is moving along. On each new film roll your consciousness enters the next version of the mannequin, which then comes to life and becomes you in the current frame.

The mannequin can change right now, in a short period of time. You are capable of changing very quickly, to the point of spectacularly changing your outer appearance. You can also change qualities and skills such as: self-confidence, charm, ability to communicate, courage, intelligence, and professionalism.

Changing yourself doesn't mean rejection of self or completely getting rid of the old you. We are talking about development. Especially if you are a rare exception of someone who likes themselves the way they are and doesn't particularly feel the need to change themselves. But even if that is the case, you have to keep developing, otherwise you'll go down the route of deterioration. *You need to change yourself, without changing yourself, your core identity, your fundamental principles, convictions and philosophy of life.*

Uniqueness *Uniqueness is all you have, but to a great extent, this is more than enough. Uniqueness is perfect unto itself because there is nothing of its kind anywhere else.* Is it valuable, that which cannot be found anywhere else in anyone else? Undoubtedly. It is an advantage, which you can either use or chuck to the back of a dusty cupboard. And it is all a matter of choice.

But all shortcomings have one paradoxical aspect. If you accept a shortcoming, it becomes a valuable, individual quality. If you don't accept a shortcoming and battle against it, the shortcoming becomes a flaw. This is exactly how others will perceive it: either as a valuable quality, or as a flaw. *If you accept a personal shortcoming, it can transform into an advantage.*

You are perfect, just as Nature and the Creator intended you to be. *Perfection is when an individual is embodying their uniqueness and in harmony with the self.* Where there is acceptance, harmony appears. And the opposite is true; any negation gives rise to disharmony, which everyone notices.

An obvious vice or weak point that directly harms you, your health, and reputation for example, or that harms others, should be rooted out. In everything else though, it is better to develop your positive qualities *than to battle with your shortcomings.*

The three achievements method *First,* don't focus on your shortcomings. *Don't dwell on feeling deprived in some way;* this is a destructive state. Your shortcomings will only worsen and this will lead to greater deterioration. You have to shift into a different, more constructive state. This will help with the second action.

Second. You have to have a goal in life — something inspiring that fills you with enthusiasm, that benefits you and others. If you feel apathetic about life in general, then, you don't have a goal. Or, if you look at it from the other way around — when you have no goal, you feel apathetic about life. If you have no goal, you won't have anything to desire. If you experience no sense of striving — there will be no movement in your life. No movement, no energy; no energy, no life. So, you must find your true goal, *your life purpose*, *and begin moving towards it*. Without a life purpose, whatever that might be, there is no 'you'; you are an empty space. If you haven't yet found a life purpose, the third action will help you.

Third. Whether you have found your life purpose or not, you should concentrate on personal development, *on re-making yourself*. Focus on yourself constantly, always. Kindle in yourself the Creator's Spark, work on self-development and self-improvement. This method delivers three achievements instantly: shake off a state of feeling deprived, find your life purpose, realise your life purpose.

Triple action Goals are achieved via triple action: propel reality, propel yourself, propel yourself from within. Self-development is a worthy goal and path. Your life purpose on this path will find itself. Once you have found it, there should be no stopping you. Remember: there is either development or deterioration.

You mustn't think of self-development as an onerous duty or heavy chore. Quite the opposite, it's much harder to experience stagnation, inactivity, and laziness. *Working on yourself is no labour but pleasant preparation for something more pleasant.* For you to get ready when you are going to a party, don't you smarten yourself up? The party is today. A one-time preparation won't be enough for what will come tomorrow, in a month's time or in a year from now.

Your life purpose Your life purpose is what inspires you and benefits yourself and others. To become magnificent and turn your life into magnificence, you have to shift out of a state of stagnation and degradation. The way out is to find your life purpose, your true goal, and then take steps towards it. Your life purpose is your course of self-realisation. Without a life purpose, life turns into a mindless existence. You may not be aware of what your life purpose is. The Creator's Spark that smoulders inside you **knows**. *But it has to be kindled.* By kindling inside the Creator's Spark, working on yourself, you achieve these three things: you leave stagnation behind, you find your life purpose, you realise your life purpose.

Occupying a new mannequin Let's say you want to have a beautiful body, transform yourself into a charming personality, pleasant in all respects, or become a high-paid professional in a particular field. Essentially, this means to occupy your *perfected mannequin on a fundamentally different film roll*. Have no doubt that this film roll and such a mannequin exists. All you have to do is get there. This goal is achieved via triple action: propel reality, propel yourself, propel yourself from within. See chapter 'You are brilliant', 'The Imitation Technique' etc.

* * *

This overview gives the basics. To assimilate all the subtle details of this material, you will need to read the whole book very carefully. If there is something that you do not understand, read the book about Transurfing. Transurfing is essentially primary school. By comparison, Tufti's techniques are high school and aerobatics.

Other books you may find helpful include:

Transurfing Reality — the basics explained — how reality works and what to do with it.

Separate Reality Projector — A detailed description and tool for creating and equipping your personal world.

Hacking The Technogenic System — How not to become a cog in the matrix.

'kLIBE' — *The End of The Illusion of the Herd Mentality* — How to survive in a technogenic environment and achieve set goals.

'cleanEating' — How to get back to a healthy, fit body.

Printed in Great Britain
by Amazon

35912596R00118